Praise for *Adap*

"Now, more than ever, educators need practical and actionable strategies that they can use in their classrooms. While teaching is incredibly complex, by learning with colleagues and applying the research, all educators can improve their practice and help all children achieve new heights in learning and outcomes. In this new book, Jonathan Ryan Davis and Maureen Connolly have applied their own expertise and that of researchers and practitioners in such a way that all educators can benefit. You'll find their strategies to be clear, applicable, and exactly what our educators need right now in order to ensure that all schools are great places for both students and adults to thrive."

—Dr. Joshua P. Starr, CEO of PDK International

"This book offers a wealth of strategies, inspirations, and practical suggestions to provide support and guidance in the never-ending pursuit of strengthening teaching and learning. This isn't just a 'how-to-book,' it is a 'this is how I have done it' book that offers teacher-developed, research-backed, easy-to-adapt practices that will be valuable to teachers who are new to the field and to all teachers striving to meet the needs of each student. Written with respect for teachers and an appreciation of the unique qualities of each classroom, *Adaptable Teaching: 30 Practical Strategies for All School Contexts* will build the toolbox of individual teachers and provide opportunities for rich professional discussion and collaboration. I cannot wait to dig into this book and series with my colleagues."

—Mary Eldredge-Sandbo, EdD, NBCT,
2010 North Dakota Teacher of the Year

Adaptable Teaching

About the *Building Your Teaching Toolbox* Book Series

We chose to name this series "Building Your Teaching Toolbox" because we think a toolbox is a strong metaphor for becoming an effective educator. New teachers enter the profession with a toolbox that needs to be filled with strategies they can try out and practice in order to determine which are their "go-to" tools. Veteran teachers often have a teaching toolbox filled with some tools that are well worn and others that might be in need of revitalizing or updating to make them more efficient and fun to use, and thus more useful for students.

The importance of a well-filled toolbox is not something we take lightly as educators with nearly a half-century of teaching combined under our belts; we continue to revisit our tools to figure out what needs to be updated and consider new strategies to add that enhance our pedagogy. Each district, school, classroom, and child is different, and from year to year, whether a teacher changes schools or not, tools a teacher uses need to be adapted to meet the needs of the new students they are teaching. Therefore, our book series is focused on "Building Your Teaching Toolbox" in order to support new teachers in developing practical teaching strategies they can adapt for any school context and to support veteran teachers in revitalizing and adding to their already established teaching toolbox.

Within this series, readers will find tried and tested teaching strategies that can be turnkeyed for any school context. The strategies in each book are developed from successful K–12 teachers from across the United States and globally. In attempting to create a book that would provide a comprehensive number of teaching tools to fill a teacher's toolbox, we realized one book would not suffice. This led to the creation of the five-book "Building Your Teaching Toolbox" Book Series that provides thirty strategies in each of four focus areas: (1) classroom climate, (2) planning, (3) instruction, and (4) professional development. The first book in the series provides five core strategies in each of these four areas and each subsequent book is focused on one pedagogical area at a time (Book #2: classroom climate, Book #3: planning, Book #4: instruction, and Book #5: professional development).

Having taught and supervised students in so many different school contexts, we knew this book series needed to emphasize how to modify core strategies in multiple ways. Therefore, every teaching strategy throughout the book series includes tips on how to adapt the strategy based on grade level, type of learner, and different school assets and needs like class size, technology, and cultural diversity.

Along with these adaptations, we wanted to be sure that readers could imagine what strategy implementation might be like in their classrooms. Each strategy comes alive through the stories of how contributing teachers have used and adapted the strategies they shared. We also recognized that one great strategy actually requires numerous tiny strategies to effectively execute; so we broke down each strategy like nesting dolls where readers will see the overall larger strategy and then more and more details are revealed that will help readers make the strategy their own.

We believe the "Building Your Teaching Toolbox" Books Series will serve as a practical resource for educators of all backgrounds and experience while also helping to create a toolbox community where we can continue to learn from and grow with one another. Thanks for becoming part of that community!

Adaptable Teaching

30 Practical Strategies for All School Contexts

Jonathan Ryan Davis and
Maureen Connolly

ROWMAN & LITTLEFIELD
Lanham • Boulder • New York • London

Published by Rowman & Littlefield
An imprint of The Rowman & Littlefield Publishing Group, Inc.
4501 Forbes Boulevard, Suite 200, Lanham, Maryland 20706
www.rowman.com

86-90 Paul Street, London EC2A 4NE, United Kingdom

British Library Cataloguing in Publication Information Available

Library of Congress Cataloging-in-Publication Data

Names: Davis, Jonathan Ryan, author. | Connolly, Maureen (English teacher), author.
Title: Adaptable teaching : 30 practical strategies for all school contexts / Jonathan Ryan Davis, Maureen Connolly.
Description: Lanham : Rowman & Littlefield, [2022] | Series: Building your teaching toolbox | Includes bibliographical references. | Summary: "This book is designed for all K–12 educators and teacher preparation faculty. Each of the strategies presented includes perspectives from teachers at two different grade levels representing a range of suburban and urban teachers"—Provided by publisher.
Identifiers: LCCN 2021050062 (print) | LCCN 2021050063 (ebook) | ISBN 9781475849721 (cloth) | ISBN 9781475849738 (paperback) | ISBN 9781475849745 (epub)
Subjects: LCSH: Teaching.
Classification: LCC LB1025.3 .D39 2022 (print) | LCC LB1025.3 (ebook) | DDC 371.102—dc23/eng/20220110
LC record available at https://lccn.loc.gov/2021050062
LC ebook record available at https://lccn.loc.gov/2021050063

∞™ The paper used in this publication meets the minimum requirements of American National Standard for Information Sciences—Permanence of Paper for Printed Library Materials, ANSI/NISO Z39.48-1992.

Foreword

Lawrence Pendergast

"Those schools that are frequently considered 'successful schools' or 'our best schools?' In those schools, education is already responsive to the students who are attending them." Dr. Christopher Emdin shared this observation at a conference we hosted, at which he was the keynote speaker. And in this simple, keenly pointed commentary, Dr. Emdin noted a profound truth: if we want our students to be successful, we need to take who they are into account, and where they are in their respective learning journeys, and shape our instructional thinking and planning and implementation accordingly.

This is easy to say, but when it comes down to it, there is an age-old question that has vexed teachers everywhere: "Ok, so how do we *do* that?" And for all the professional learning these same teachers attend (or are dragged to, or subjected to, or admonished to attend, etc.), for all the theory and research they push themselves to read closely and thoughtfully, and for all the instructional practice they engage in through cycles of continuous learning in their classrooms, teachers continue to value one source above all others when it comes to honing their pedagogy: their fellow practitioners.

Teachers, like students and caregivers, musicians and baseball players, learn best when learning from each other. Our fellow practitioners are feeling the same pressures, are working in similar conditions, and always understand that—for reasons that are not always clear—what works well in the morning with one class won't always work well after lunch in another. We frustrate, annoy, inspire, and emulate one another. We read research articles and textbooks and consider the moves a strong facilitator makes in a professional learning session, and then we look to each other as we craft these influences into professional practice. We seek resources that aspire to support us by explicitly sharing instructional strategies used by other in-service teachers and tap into instructional leadership in a way all pedagogues understand and respect. These resources don't just tell us what to think or how to think; they share how to *do*. And we all learn by *doing*.

I was not always a nameless, faceless bureaucrat: before becoming Deputy Chief Academic Officer (Division of Teaching and Learning) in the New York City Department of Education, I was a full-time teacher for over ten years in New York City. When I became an assistant principal, I continued teaching a few classes every day, and as a principal—then as an executive principal—I continued teaching a class here and there, as it is all too easy to quickly forget the unique challenges of daily classroom teaching. Students and teachers are not static—they change and evolve as people and as learners over the course of a day, a week, a month, and, of course, years. As an Executive Superintendent I used to visit classrooms and consider how knowledge gleaned from PD sessions was put into practice in classrooms, and I would notice that at the end of the day the teachers always touched base with each other about how things went and where they should go next.

Nothing is ever formulaic when it comes to impactful teaching practice because our students are always changing—so our responsiveness needs to change along with them. It takes a great deal of energy to get to the end of the teaching day and still be motivated to seek out new approaches—but the best teachers do exactly that, all the time. Jonathan Ryan Davis, Maureen Connolly, and the teachers who contributed to this book are those teachers who have taken years of learning and dedication to improving practice, and make the conscious effort every day to work with colleagues to get better.

We have been challenged over the past several years with thoughtfully and safely navigating COVID-19 and a reckoning with racial injustice to rethink how we approach teaching and learning: challenged to make our instructional materials more inclusive and reflective of all of our students, challenged to reconsider all of our assumptions about what we should expect of ourselves as teachers and our students as learners, challenged to see and respond to who our learners are as individuals and within their lived experience. We certainly have been challenged to strive to improve our long-distance pedagogy, via remote means, in times of enormous stress on our nation and its families.

The best teachers will, at times, struggle to understand where a student is finding obstacles to learning—this is all the more challenging when we can't see our students and we can't sit beside them and understand where they are on their learning journeys. And in this ever-changing instructional landscape, to continue to adapt and hone their craft, teachers met these challenges not by turning to their dust-covered textbooks, nor to webinars offered by the reigning wizards of high-tech pedagogical theory; instead, as they so often have done in the past and undoubtedly will continue to do, teachers have turned to each other.

We've all been there—we've all longed to know what someone else is doing in a classroom, wanted to know how they were thinking about approaching certain content, what activities and strategies they were developing and replicating or, at times, rejecting out of hand. We've wanted to know how our fellow teachers think and approach teaching and learning, and we've wanted to learn from them.

To do this effectively, we need our colleagues in our school buildings and our colleagues from across our districts, states, nation, and the globe to share their thinking, their planning, their approaches. *Adaptable Teaching: Thirty Practical Strategies for ALL School Contexts* provides a platform for teachers from a variety of school settings to do this.

—Lawrence Pendergast
Deputy Chief Academic Officer
(Division of Teaching and Learning)
New York City Department of Education

Acknowledgments

We are incredibly grateful to all of the teachers who contributed to this book. Our conversations with them were insightful and inspiring, and we are glad to be able to share their teacher moves with you. Each contributor is listed at the start of the chapter that they helped form. We also want to recognize all contributors together, here at the start of this book. They were the original toolbox community. We are eager for you, our readers, to join!

Jasmeen (Jazz) Aboulezz, American International School (Kuwait), 5th grade
Rebecca Austern, PS 261 (NY), 1st grade
Emilio Burgos, PS 360 Queens (NY), grades K–3rd grade
Mary Brady, Lloyd Memorial High School (KY), 10th and 12th grade
Caitlin Cahill, PS 503 (NY), Kindergarten and 5th grade
Kelsey Collins, Livingston High School (NJ), 11th and 12th grade
Janelle Chiorello, Joyce Kilmer Middle School (NJ), 8th grade
Lindsay Davis, The Baldwin School (PA), 10th and 11th grade
Rachel Field Dennis, Morris Academy for Collaborative Studies (NY), 12th grade
Diedre Downing, NYC iSchool (NY), 9th grade
Chad Frade, Urban Assembly Maker High School (NY), 9th–12th grade
Sarah Gibson, Middle School 88 (NY), 7th grade
Kaity Haley, Thomas Grover Middle School (NJ), 8th grade
Deborah Kim, PS 40 (NY), Kindergarten
Brittany Klimowicz, NYC iSchool (NY), 9th–12th grade
Jennifer (Jenn) Levi, Hampton Street School (NY), Kindergarten
Christine Mercer, Yardville Elementary School (NJ), 4th grade
Beth Merrill, Sunset High School (OR), 9th–12th grade
Naeem Muse, Luis Munoz Rivera Community Middle School (NJ), 8th grade
Kimberly Murray, Colegio Karl C. Parrish (Colombia), Kindergarten
Jeanne Muzi, Slackwood School (NJ), K–3rd grade
Katherine O'Sullivan, Bay Shore Middle School (NY), 7th grade
Meaghan Phillips, Byram Intermediate School (NJ), 5th–8th grade
Tobey Reed, Attleboro High School (MA), 9th–12th grade
Amaris Rodriguez Brown, RFK High School (NY), 11th and 12th grade

Barry Saide, Roosevelt School (NJ), 4th–5th grade
Bette Sloane, Mineola High School (NY), 8th–12th grade
Tina Tuminaro, Pond Road Middle School (NJ), 6th grade
Ashley Warren, West Windsor High School North (NJ), 9th–12th grade
Cathy Xiong, Robert F Wagner Schools for Arts and Technology (NY), 6th–8th grade

Thank you to The College of New Jersey's (TCNJ) School of Education for funding the grant that helped us write this book. Our smart and driven colleagues and friends at TCNJ made this work possible. We are grateful for such a supportive work environment.

Thank you to Sarah Reynolds, our research assistant extraordinaire! Your insight, organization, and passion made our writing process smooth and focused. These qualities are part of the many gifts you will share with your future students! Also, thank you to our research assistant team of Druscilla Kojiem, Kerry Rushnak, Joely Torres, and Sreenidhi Viswanathan for helping to shape and build the toolbox community with the launch of this first book in our series!

The book's beautiful cover art was created by the super-talented Nelly Sanchez Aranda who created an image that brilliantly represents the essence and content of this book and our entire *Building Your Teaching Toolbox Book Series*.

Thank you to the teachers and students who inspired this book! We are humbled by your commitment to teaching and learning, and we hope this book serves as a solid resource for you.

Last, but not least, thank you to our families. Andrew, Anna, and Ben—Maureen appreciates your patience, support, and constant inspiration! Becca, Zola, and Kai—Jonathan is grateful for your unwavering love and support that inspired this book and so much more. We are excited to see how this book can impact and influence Zola, Kai, Ben, and Anna's future teachers!

Introduction

Thank you for reading our book! We are excited about connecting with our readers and providing support to you as educators. As you read this book, consider how you can adapt these strategies to fit the needs of your students and your own needs as a teacher. If you have some great stories about how you have used these strategies, please connect with us!

Website: https://buildyourteachingtoolbox.com/, Email: buildyourteachingtoolbox@gmail.com, Twitter: @BuildTeachTool, Instagram: @buildteachingtoolbox, TikTok: @buildteachingtoolbox, Facebook: Build Your Teaching Toolbox.

We are eager for this book to engage readers in "upping" their teaching skills and deepening their commitment to this profession. Read on for new ideas and inspiration!

WHO WE ARE

Years ago, we met as professors of education at The College of New Jersey (TCNJ) where we instantly bonded over our love of P-12 teaching and collaborating with pre- and in-service teachers. Our teaching backgrounds represent varied experiences and teaching contexts, which instigated a dialogue that resulted in this book. Outside of TCNJ, we are also part of the CBK Associates team of consultants working with Youth Leadership Councils in New York City.

Jonathan's teaching career began as a high school social studies teacher at Lloyd Memorial High School, a low-income, public high school in northern Kentucky, where he taught for three years. He then moved to teach in New York City for four years in two separate, Title I, public schools: Urban Assembly School of Design and Construction (Manhattan high school) and Eagle Academy for Young Men at Ocean Hill (Brooklyn 6–12 school). Jonathan taught Global History, New York State Regents and Advanced Placement (AP) US History, Government, Economics, and a course on Race in America. Jonathan was also an adjunct professor for four years at John Jay College, Hunter College, and Brooklyn College, where he taught courses in education, pedagogy, and sociology. During his decade plus of teaching before becoming a professor of education, Jonathan served as a department chair, instructional coach, and field supervisor for student teachers. At TCNJ, where he coordinates the Urban Secondary Education Program, he focuses his research and practice on culturally responsive and sustaining pedagogy—specifically on how to adapt strategies to support the needs of all types of learners in all types of settings. Jonathan recently published his book *Classroom Management in Teacher Education Programs* (Palgrave Macmillan).

Maureen taught for fifteen years at Mineola High School, a public high school in a middle class, suburban town on Long Island, New York. There, she taught New York State Regents examination support, inclusion, and AP English classes. The range in abilities among her students made her realize the importance of sharing and gathering strong and successful lesson ideas with colleagues. Maureen was also the coordinator for Service Learning for the New York Metropolitan area and worked at Queens College, Molloy College, and Adelphi University as an adjunct professor of education. She has provided professional development (PD) focused on service learning and literacy across the United States and in several other countries. Maureen has published three books: *Getting to the Core of English Language Arts, Grades 6–12* (Corwin); *Getting to the Core of Literacy for History/Social Studies, Science, and Technical Subjects, Grades 6–12* (Corwin); and *Next Generation Literacy: Using the Tests (You Think) You Hate to Help the Students you Love* (ASCD). Maureen's research and practice is focused on practical strategies and planning that support students' application of knowledge and skills to issues that matter to them.

As teacher educators and consultants, our passion, teaching, and research are focused on practical, pedagogical methods to support the needs of pre-service and in-service teachers.

WHY WE WROTE THIS BOOK

When working with our teacher candidates, we have consistently been asked for more strategies that will make them effective teachers. The cooperating teachers with whom we work are also eager to diversify the approaches they take in their classrooms. We have utilized several different books in our classes, and in leading PD, with the intention of "filling" teachers' toolboxes with strategies; however, many of the teachers we work with do not believe the strategies they read about can translate to their school and classroom contexts. As a result, we were inspired to create a book that can account for the pedagogical needs of teachers working in *varied* school and community contexts through a culturally responsive/sustaining lens.

The reality is that teachers can be masters of their content, brilliant lesson designers, and plan the most amazing projects; yet, if they are unable to connect with the students, they will usually not be effective in the classroom. That is why Gloria Ladson-Billings and Geneva Gay helped pioneer this approach to teaching that utilizes culturally relevant practices to help students succeed. Ladson-Billings (1995) coined the term culturally relevant pedagogy (CRP): "a theoretical model that not only addresses student achievement but also helps students to accept and affirm their cultural identity while developing critical perspectives that challenge inequities that schools (and other institutions) perpetuate" (p. 469). As a theoretical model, educators began to think about what this looked like in practice. Therefore, Geneva Gay (2000) extended the application of Ladson-Billings by focusing the application of culturally relevant pedagogy through what she termed culturally responsive teaching (CRT), which is "using the cultural knowledge, prior experiences, frames of reference, and performance styles of ethnically diverse students to make learning encounters more relevant to and effective for them" (p. 31).

Moving toward CRT was a positive step in helping teachers integrate culturally responsive and relevant practices; but as critical educators began to apply CRP and CRT, they realized it is not enough to integrate culturally responsive and relevant pedagogy into their practice: the work in the classroom should be culturally *sustaining* for students (CSP). As a result, Django Paris and H. Samy Alim (2017) focused on the ways teachers can take into account, draw on, and sustain how students' identities and cultures evolve. And we cannot forget, as Irizarry (2007) pointed out, "culture is not a fixed entity, but rather always changing; a diversity of experiences exists even among members of the same cultural group. If a teacher follows a checklist of behaviors that have been attributed to a specific cultural group, he or she can reinforce stereotypes and actually do more harm than good" (p. 23). We need to be responsive and reflective of our students' backgrounds and cultures, work toward sustaining them, as well as not fall into the trap of thinking all students from the same culture are the same.

For this book, we embrace CRP, CRT, and CSP; we use the term culturally responsive/sustaining teaching (CRT) throughout this text as a representation of the synthesis of these approaches. We acknowledge that to truly embody these responsive and sustaining practices, it is also important that we, as educators, consider the *whole child* and extend our work outside of the classroom. As ASCD (2007) advocated:

> We call on communities—educators, parents, businesses, health and social service providers, arts professionals, recreation leaders, and policymakers at all levels—to forge a new compact with our young people to ensure their whole and healthy development. We ask communities to redefine learning to focus on the whole person. We ask schools and communities to lay aside perennial battles for resources and instead align those resources in support of the whole child. Policy, practice, and resources must be aligned to support not only academic learning for each child, but also the experiences that encourage development of a whole child—one who is knowledgeable, healthy, motivated, and engaged. (ASCD, 2007, p. 8)

We use culturally responsive/sustaining practices and consider the whole child throughout this book because, even as CRT has become more commonly known across educational circles, many teachers struggle to take these theories and concepts and put them into practice. We have continually heard teachers ask: How can I make this work in *my* classroom? How does this apply to *my* students, in *my* school? This book was created to help answer those questions, as we focus on how each strategy can be adapted to meet varied school and classroom contexts.

KEY CONCEPTS TO CONSIDER

Understanding by Design (UbD)

UbD is a key framework that is woven throughout this book. This framework consists of three stages:

Stage 1: Desired Results—What do you want your students to know and be able to do?
Stage 2: Evidence—How will you measure students' progress toward desired results?
Stage 3: Instruction—What will you and your students do to engage in meaningful learning experiences that help them meet desired results?

Wiggins and McTighe (2004) describe the process of working through the framework:

> Plan with the "end in mind" by first clarifying the learning you seek; that is, the desired learning results (Stage 1). Then, think about the evidence needed to certify that students have achieved those desired learnings (Stage 2). Finally, plan the means to the end; that is, the teaching and learning activities and resources to help students achieve the goals (Stage 3). (p. 25)

Wiggins and McTighe (2004) also make clear that this is a framework, not a linear, step-by-step process for planning: "Curriculum design is not only idiosyncratic but also iterative. Although there is a clear logic embodied in the three stages of backward design, the process is not rigidly linear or step-by-step" (p. 4).

Knowledge, Skills, Dispositions (K/S/D)

When thinking about desired results, we consider three interrelated areas for students to grow:

1. *Knowledge*—The concepts that you want students to understand and think about critically
2. *Skills*—Ways you want students to be able to work with this knowledge
3. *Dispositions*—Attitudes toward learning and social interaction that you want students to cultivate

Thinking about desired results becomes clearer when we consider K/S/D. Sometimes we get caught up in content and lose the consideration of skills and dispositions that students need in order to think critically about that content. Sometimes, we try to teach a skill and realize that students do not have the knowledge to apply that skill yet. Still other times, we see our students running out of energy or perseverance or not knowing how to communicate their needs clearly because of impatience or frustration. This can signal a need for dispositional shifts. If we have the language to describe what we want students to be able to do and what students need in order to do it, we will be clearer in communicating with them and supporting them.

That being said, it can be difficult to decide which category best fits a particular desired result. For example, is learning long division a matter of K/S/D? We would argue that it is all three. A student must have basic numerical sense (knowledge), apply that sense to computational thinking (skill), and persevere in developing further understanding and skills in order to apply them to more complex problems (disposition). We want to stress that it is important to consider K/S/D, but not get caught up in designating which category fits your objectives or desired results best.

We also need to remember that students typically forget the content we teach them, but the skills and dispositions they develop in our classrooms endure. Therefore, we stress the integration of K/S/D development throughout your teaching to help prepare and develop the whole child and productive, participatory members of our communities.

Assessment

The word *assess* comes from the Latin root assidēre "to sit next to or by." To assess calls for teachers to sit beside students and understand where they are in their learning, in order to help them move forward. Unfortunately, assessment has become associated with high-stakes, high-pressure, and high-anxiety rather than a means for better understanding what students need for most educators and students. If we can focus more on the idea of evidence of learning (as described in UbD), perhaps we can get back to the root of this word and a spirit of assessment that is meaningful and helpful for students and teachers.

Differentiation

Throughout this book, we make reference to opportunities for differentiation. When you differentiate, you create options for students to be successful. There are six main entry points for differentiation:

1. *Content*: knowledge and skills that students are developing
2. *Process*: means by which students use key skills to make sense of essential ideas and information
3. *Product*: ways that students demonstrate what they have learned
4. *Readiness*: level of understanding or skill
5. *Interest*: affinity, curiosity, or passion for a particular topic or skill
6. *Learning modality*: preferred method of learning

(McTighe & Tomlinson, 2008)

Differentiation can be considered during planning, on the spot while working with students, and after instruction in order to plan for next steps.

HOW THIS BOOK IS ORGANIZED

This book is framed by two overarching questions:

1. What pedagogical strategies have a positive impact on students' learning experiences and the classroom environment?
2. How can we, the authors, make the intricacies of each pedagogical strategy tangible for novice and experienced teachers working in different settings with varied learners?

To address these questions, we focus on four key areas of teaching:

1. Classroom Climate
2. Planning
3. Instruction
4. Professional Development

We focus on these four key areas because we think they encapsulate the main domains of teaching. We begin with *Classroom Climate* because it helps set the foundation for successful learning. Within the *Classroom Climate* section, we include strategies related to setting up, being responsive, and honoring student input.

We then examine different approaches to *Planning*. Within the *Planning* section, we include strategies you can use: before the school year starts, in collaboration with colleagues, to help with aligning your practice, and when transitioning from planning to practice. These strategies complement one another as they are grounded in UbD and support preparation for clear and impactful desired results.

With a culturally responsive/sustaining classroom climate established and strong ideas for planning considered, we move on to *Instruction*. Throughout the *Instruction* section, our focus is on how to help you move away from a teacher-centered model of teaching toward acting as a facilitator of learning. This includes stretching beyond your comfort zone with new ideas and approaches, increasing student-centered learning, and using assessment and feedback to inform next steps.

We conclude with our *Professional Development* section so you can think about how you can continue to grow as an educator. This includes critical reflection on your own work as a professional, developing your school community and professional network, considering your teaching disposition, and working on yourself (as a teacher and person).

Within each teaching area, we provide step-by-step instructions for applying the strategy. To help readers envision the strategy further, we provide narratives of the *Strategy in Action*. We also quote teachers explaining why they like each strategy.

We give examples of how to modify each strategy based on related assets and needs, such as technology, cultural diversity, student dispositions (introverts/extroverts), and access to resources. We also provide suggestions for modifications based on where you may be in your career (early career/veteran), what grade level you teach (elementary, middle, high), and different populations of students (Special Education, English Language Learners, and Gifted and Talented).

As you read through strategy descriptions and professional anecdotes and commentary, we hope that you will feel like a part of a larger community of educators who are eager to share and grow together.

But wait, there's more! In addition to the twenty strategies described in the four main sections, we include a list of ten more simple-to-implement strategies. We describe these strategies as being a light lift on your part with a heavy impact for your students.

WHY THIS BOOK IS FOR *ALL* TEACHERS

Our work with teachers spans multiple states and countries and connects us with varied school environments. We decided to capitalize on this diversity by developing a book that will help increase the tools teachers can use with their students and help teachers to make mindful decisions about when and how to use those tools based on their students' learning needs.

Research shows that teacher preparation must help pre-service teachers develop an array of strategies *and* the ability to reflect on each strategy according to their given setting in order to plan on how best to proceed (Darling-Hammond, 2015). We believe that this is good practice for *all* educators, regardless of where they are in their careers. This book is intended to both introduce teacher candidates and novice teachers to new strategies and to provide support for the growth and reflective practice of more seasoned teachers.

OUR CONTRIBUTORS

We are incredibly grateful to the thirty teachers who contributed to this book. We were fortunate to gather information from educators across six states (NY, PA, NJ, MA, KT, OR) and three countries (USA, Kuwait, Colombia). Our contributors represent a balance of urban (fourteen teachers) and suburban (sixteen teachers) settings as well as a range of experience in elementary, middle, and high school.

In preparation for the interview process, we asked each contributor to share information regarding their school setting. On the next page, we list the percentage of contributors who chose each descriptor as a match for their school. In some categories, you will note that the number of contributors does not equal thirty. This is because some contributors believed their school fell somewhere in the middle of the descriptors. You can see there is a wide range of assets and needs in the schools for these teachers and their students, which inform the strategies within this book.

It was heartening to hear from our contributors that the experience of being interviewed helped them remember and reinforce good strategies. The experience of developing this book reminded us of tried and tested approaches or informed us of new approaches to use in our own teaching. For this collaboration and inspiration from teacher contributors, we are more grateful than our words can express.

Contributors' School Contexts: Assets and Needs

Assets	*Needs*
My students don't worry about money for basic needs (food, clothing, etc.). - 62% (16 teachers).	My students are distracted by concerns about money for basic needs (food, clothing, etc.). - 38% (10 teachers).
My students have access to technology inside and outside the classroom. - 72% (21 teachers).	My students do not have access to technology in the classroom or at home. - 28% (8 teachers).
My classroom population represents a range of racial and ethnic diversity. - 55% (16 teachers).	My classroom community is homogeneous in terms of racial and ethnic diversity. - 45% (13 teachers).
My class sizes are small. - 48% (12 teachers).	My class sizes are large. - 52% (13 teachers).
Students consistently attend school. - 89% (25 teachers).	Students do not consistently attend school - 11% (3 teachers).
My day is structured to allow time for individual instruction/feedback. - 59% (16 teachers).	I rarely have time for individual instruction/ feedback. - 41% (11 teachers).
My school provides and makes time for quality professional development. - 68% (19 teachers).	I do not have access to quality professional development. - 32% (9 teachers).
My school values interdisciplinary learning. - 74% (20 teachers).	My school does not value interdisciplinary learning. - 26% (7 teachers).
I have strong relationships and consistent contact with my students' parents/guardians. - 76% (19 teachers).	I have no relationship or interactions with my students' parents/guardians. - 24% (6 teachers).
My students want to learn and see that good grades are a result of their learning. - 54% (13 teachers).	My students are more focused on good grades, than actual learning. - 46% (11 teachers).

FINAL WORDS

We hope you will be inspired to use the strategies you find in the following pages. We've worked to share the structure of these strategies and to answer questions you might have through our detailed, step-by-step overviews. Teaching and learning is about trying new ideas and approaches. We want to encourage you to keep up your momentum!

Chapter 1

Classroom Climate Strategies

This chapter explores the following classroom climate strategies:

- Creating *Group Agreements* to set norms for interactions and behaviors in the classroom (Strategy 1)
- *Establishing Routines* that help you and your students create your desired classroom environment (Strategy 2)
- Using *Positive Affirmations* to recognize the behavioral and/or academic accomplishments of students either publicly or privately (Strategy 3)
- Helping students *Fail Forward* by looking at mistakes in order to grow from what has happened (Strategy 4)
- Incorporating *Critical Feedback Surveys* to elicit feedback from students on specific learning activities, assessment, and/or other classroom experiences (Strategy 5)

The strategies in this chapter are organized, in a sense, chronologically so you can begin by establishing group agreements (Strategy 1), and then move into creating solid routines (Strategy 2), which will be reinforced by integrating positive affirmations throughout your lessons (Strategy 3). Next, because of the strong culture established as a result of Strategies 1, 2, and 3, you are able to implement failing forward strategies (Strategy 4) before relying on critical feedback surveys (Strategy 5) to evaluate how you and your students can continue to improve and develop your classroom learning environment.

HELPFUL UNDERSTANDINGS

This chapter utilizes larger frames and ideas that you will see referenced often.

Maslow before You Can Bloom

At the ASCD Empower19 Conference in Chicago, Mr. Dwayne Reed (2019) centered his keynote address around the statement, "You gotta Maslow before you can Bloom," a catchphrase that highlighted the relationship between Maslow's (1943) hierarchy of needs and Bloom's Taxonomy (1956). This quote has been used for over a decade by educators like Tomaz Lasic (2009) and Jake Miller (2016) to emphasize that teachers must help students meet their physiological and safety needs before they can achieve love and belonging, esteem, and self-actualization. Only when basic needs are met, can students truly embark on Bloom's Taxonomy where they start by building a foundation of knowledge and understanding and move toward higher-level application, analysis, synthesis, and evaluation.

The strategies in this chapter embrace meeting the hierarchy of needs of students before challenging students to tackle Bloom's Taxonomy, which you will also see in the subsequent chapters of this book.

Maslow before You Can Bloom Highlights

- See how to get students to feel comfortable in your classroom *before day 1* in *Establishing Routines* (Strategy 2).
- Learn about how *Positive Affirmations* (Strategy 3) can directly support students who struggle with low self-esteem.
- Explore the social-emotional foundations for *Failing Forward* (Strategy 4) used in an elementary school classroom.

Dynamic Classroom Management Approach (DCMA)

The DCMA was created to get teachers to reenvision what classroom management means and focus on creating positive classroom learning environments. DCMA is broken into four domains: Flexibility, Diversity, Pedagogy, and Classroom Culture and Community (Davis, 2017), which collectively help teachers engage their students and create optimal learning environments where each student feels supported, challenged, and seen. For DCMA to work optimally, teachers must think critically about how they can best create positive classroom learning environments and adapt those strategies to meet the needs of each student they teach.

In the strategies that follow in this chapter, you will read about ways to dynamically think about establishing the classroom climate you want for your students.

DCMA Highlights

- Explore how a "Class Jigsaw Puzzle" can establish a community from the first week of the year in *Group Agreements* (Strategy 1).
- Uncover "Base Groups" in *Establishing Routines* (Strategy 2), which challenge students to work collaboratively throughout the year.
- Learn how you can build a classroom community in an elementary English Language classroom using *Positive Affirmations* (Strategy 3).
- Consider throwing a "Failing Forward Party" as described in *Failing Forward* (Strategy 4).

- See how "Plus/Deltas" in *Critical Feedback Surveys* (Strategy 5) can help individuals and classes be open and grow together.

Culturally Responsive/Sustaining Teaching

As highlighted in the introduction, each strategy in this book is guided by culturally responsive/sustaining teaching (CRT). Complementing the work done with DCMA, CRT lays its foundation in helping to support teachers in creating positive classroom climates. For each strategy in this chapter, look for ways students are at the center of choices being made in the classroom and students are equal participants in those decisions. Once you are able to support students in taking ownership of their own learning and empower themselves, you will be able to take academic risks together in the classroom.

GUIDING QUESTIONS

As you read through this chapter, consider the following:

- How am I creating an environment in which my students "Maslow" before they "Bloom"?
- What elements of DCMA can I consistently integrate into my classroom?
- How can I collaboratively create group agreements within my classroom?
- What routines are best to establish in my classroom to help create my ideal classroom environment?
- How can positive affirmations become a consistent part of my daily lessons? How will I ensure all of my students receive positive affirmations weekly?
- What do I need to do in order to support my students with failing forward?
- What kind of critical feedback surveys will be most effective with my students?

STRATEGY 1: GROUP AGREEMENTS

Chapter Contributors
Deborah Kim, PS 40 (NY), Kindergarten
Jasmeen (Jazz) Aboulezz, American International School (Kuwait), 5th grade

Group Agreements set norms for interactions and behaviors in the classroom. Based on shared values, teachers and students develop mutually beneficial and acceptable expectations that promote a strong classroom community and a safe space for learning.

STRATEGY IMPLEMENTATION

To successfully develop lasting group agreements, students and teachers need to recognize that behaviors, whether expected or unexpected, cause other people around them to feel a corresponding way (e.g., calm/happy when you do an "expected" behavior or scared/upset when you do an "unexpected" behavior). With that in mind, consider how your choices and behavior impact the way the classroom environment functions and supports shared values.

1. *Establish the Classroom as a Community*—A community works together to promote good for all. Help your students see themselves as part of a community by:
   - Creating a visual that represents their classroom community. This visual should include all students' and teacher(s)' names. (See Figure 1.1)
   - Discussing how the visual represents important shared values such as:
     - Opportunities to share and to listen
     - Trust
     - Time for independent work
     - Group work
     - Multiple voices in the curriculum
2. *Chart and Discuss Expected/Unexpected Behaviors*—Sharing examples of expected and unexpected behaviors helps students visualize positive choices and consider how to respond when they do not follow the agreements.
   - Create a T-Chart with "expected behaviors" and "unexpected behaviors"
   - Share visuals and/or written examples of different behaviors on cards
   - Students place the cards in the appropriate category
   - Discuss the situation described

Sample Expected/Unexpected Behaviors

Expected Behavior: Raising your hand
Discussion: Why is this important?
Possible Response: Most students are used to talking whenever they want outside of school and may not consider others' feelings of wanting a turn or wanting some wait time to think.
Unexpected Behavior: Pushing another person
Discussion: Why might the student choose to act this way?
Possible Response: Frustration, excitement, and so on.
Next Steps: Check that no one is hurt; discuss why this happened; genuine apology

3. *Collaborate to Develop a List of Written Agreements*—When developing group agreements, be sure to know WHY you are including each agreement on your list. Reasons for agreements could include safety, time management, empathy, and/or increased learning. For each agreement:
   - Start by stating WHY the expected behavior is important (e.g., we value all students' voices, so we will stay quiet and attentive when another student is talking and we will share the "microphone" by staying aware of how long we are talking). See Figure 1.2.
   - Discuss each proposed agreement and adapt as needed until the class approves it.
   - Record the decided upon agreement (on a large paper, online, or both).

> Stay Positive!
> State all agreements in the positive. Focus on what you will be doing rather than on what to avoid.

4. *What Happens If . . .*—Before finalizing your group agreements, it is important to consider what could happen if an agreement is not followed. To do this:
   - Go through each agreement, one at a time, to determine implications and next steps for not following the agreement.
   - Make notes next to each agreement that break down the "what happens if." See Figure 1.3.
5. *Finalize the Group Agreements*—After you have added the "what happens if," review the group agreements one more time and, if everyone is in agreement, have each person (you included) sign the agreements and post them around the classroom (physically and/or digitally).
6. *Revisit Group Agreements*—After some time, review the agreements to ensure they are still relevant. Make changes as needed. If an agreement is not followed, you will need to revisit it. Use these steps:
   1. Look at group agreements together to determine which agreement wasn't followed.
   2. Consider whether the agreement needs to be revised, and if so, how.

3. Discuss as a class what next steps you can take to support classmates' positive choices as related to the agreement.
4. Create an action plan to promote positive choices and sticking to the agreement.

How to Apologize

Students may need guidance for developing an apology when they do not adhere to group agreements. Apologies typically have three parts:

1. Admitting wrongdoing (I'm sorry for . . .)
2. Recognizing the effect of the wrongdoing (I realize that it made you feel . . .)
3. Making amends by planning to make better choices (In the future, I will . . .)

CONSIDERING DIFFERENT TYPES OF LEARNERS

Group agreements can be adapted for different types of learners:

1. *English Language Learners* might share words in their base languages that connect with the rationale for the agreement or the expected behavior.
2. *Special Education* students may be excellent at using their divergent thinking skills to think of ways that an agreement would not be followed and what to do next.
3. *Gifted and Talented* students may benefit from considering the perspective of students who struggle. This is particularly important when considering the amount of time that they "share the mic" or give space/time for other students to talk.

STRATEGY IN ACTION: GLITCH/BUMMER/DISASTER

"When an agreement isn't followed, it is likely going to cause a glitch or be a bummer for you and your students. Hopefully, it will not be a disaster! Introduce this language and use it regularly to model for students.

1. Create a visual that represents three categories of situations:
   - *Glitch*—A temporary setback that is fairly easy to solve
   - *Bummer*—A more intense setback that may take some time to get over
   - *Disaster*—Requires intervention of experts like firefighters or doctors
2. Discuss—What one student considers a 'glitch' may feel like a 'bummer' to another student.

The Glitch, Bummer, Disaster Chart is great for all kids, but especially kids who need help modifying their reactions when things go wrong. It teaches them to have some perspective on their problems and that their reaction should match the severity of the problem. Therefore, instead of getting extremely upset over a lost pencil, kids realize that it's only a glitch and the solution is to simply get another pencil. The students also learn to use this language with each other throughout the day."

—*Deborah Kim*

How to Implement the Strategy at Varied Grade Levels

Elementary	*Middle*	*High*
*Use pictures or drawings to represent agreements and examples of expected/unexpected behavior.	*Encourage open conversation about what is happening in adolescence that makes it difficult to abide by group agreements. *Create opportunities for anonymous responses to questions regarding values and/or desired group agreements in order to avoid influence of peer pressure.	*Consider how to balance "playing by the rules" with being true to yourself. If an agreement or expectation is in conflict with a student's values, be prepared to discuss and possibly adapt that expectation.

Adaptation for Different Assets/Needs

Time	
Limited Time	*Lots of Time*
*Include reference to agreements and language that helps clarify (e.g., glitch, bummer, disaster) in your classroom talk. *Once a week or once a month, students use an emoji to represent how well the class is following and respecting group agreements.	*Host daily morning meetings during which a portion of the time is used for students to check in on how they are following and respecting group agreements and whether any of the agreements need revising. *Learn about group agreements in other classrooms. Are there any you would like to share? If there are agreements that seem positive for the entire school culture, consider revising the school handbook to reflect them.
Cultural Diversity	
Limited Diversity	*Lots of Diversity*
*Have students consider what would work for others who might have different values/needs. *Tap into areas where students may not be similar. For instance, they still have different opinions about "little things" like which soccer team is better. Can they discuss this while adhering to the group agreements?	*Create and support a culture of acceptance. (See Strategy 10: Culturally Responsive/Sustaining Teaching.) *Check in often: • What is happening? • Why is it happening? • Does it align with our agreements? • If not, how do students know how to say, "I was wrong," and how to apologize.

WHY I LIKE THIS STRATEGY

"Building the foundation of an accepting community encourages students to see beyond their opinions and open themselves up to the opportunity to learn more about others. Students learn how to deal with emotional difficulties by feeling safe and comfortable within a classroom of acceptance and tolerance."

—Jazz Aboulezz

"Discussing and establishing group agreements helps all members of the classroom community (students and teachers) link feelings to a behavior to make the cause and effect clearer. This sets us up for thinking before reacting."

—Deborah Kim

STRATEGY IN ACTION: DEFINING EXPECTATIONS TOGETHER

"One time this past year, I found that my students were struggling with the concept of being kind to one another. There were multiple cases where my students would use unkind language and become physically aggressive over what was being said by others. In seeing this and hearing the issues that my students were having, I decided to dedicate one of our morning meetings to exploring the International Baccalaureate learner profile of 'Caring.' We sat in a circle on the carpet in my classroom and, on a big chart paper, I wrote the word caring in the center of the paper for all to see. I began by explaining the reason why this word was the centerpiece of that day's morning meeting.

As I explained the reasoning behind the premise, I could see students nodding in agreement that this needed to happen. I began by modeling for my students what I was looking for by asking out loud, 'What does the word "caring" look like?' I then gave them some time to think and hands began to go up. I proceeded by giving the example of, 'To me, it looks like somebody listening to me when I am upset.' With that example given, students started to offer their own ideas and we created a class *Wordle* based on their ideas. It subsequently led to a student-driven initiative to color and design it so we could put it up on the wall. This helped students see what caring looks like and how we navigate our moments of anger and frustrations."

—Jazz Aboulezz

SAMPLE MATERIALS

Figure 1.1 Class Jigsaw Puzzle. *Source*: Jazz Aboulezz.

Group Agreements

We value…..	So we agree to….
Example: *All students' voices.*	• *Stay quiet and attentive when another student is talking* • *Share the "microphone"* • Stay *aware of how long we are talking*

Figure 1.2 Group Agreements. *Source*: Author created.

What Happens If…?

If a person…	We will…
Example: *Speaks when it is not their turn.*	• *Remind them to wait by pointing to the speaker.* • *Understand if it is because they are so excited to share.*

Figure 1.3 What Happens If . . . ? *Source*: Author created.

STRATEGY 2: ESTABLISHING ROUTINES

Chapter Contributors
Jennifer (Jenn) Levi, Hampton Street School (NY), Kindergarten
Beth Merrill, Sunset HS (OR), 9th–12th grade

Establishing Routines is a strategy that begins before the first day of school. Teachers start by thinking about their ideal classroom environment and what routines must be established to create that environment. Then, beginning on the first day of school (or before), teachers work collaboratively with their students to review, adapt, and add routines they will practice and maintain throughout the year. Routines can be focused on transitions, instruction, classroom agreements, or any other critical part of the classroom environment.

STRATEGY IMPLEMENTATION

1. *Determine the Classroom Environment/Culture You Want*—Every classroom is unique. Therefore, it is important to think about the classroom environment and culture you want within your classroom. This includes:
   - *Tone upon Entering*—Do you want students getting right to work? Do you want time for a check-in?
   - *Level of Shared Teacher-Student Leadership*—Will you determine all next steps or will students have a voice in routines/decisions?
   - *Daily Structure*—Do you want consistency or do you want to mix up the routine?
   - *Tone while Engaged in Learning*—Are you OK with chatter as long as students are productive? Are there times when the room should be silent?
   - *Closing Time Together*—How do you ensure students are thinking about the learning that took place?

2. *Figure Out What Routines Are Necessary to Enact Your Desired Environment/Culture*—Each part of your desired environment/culture can be created and maintained by developing routines that are easy to understand, engage the students, and develop buy-in by the entire class. Begin by:
   - Jotting down each component of your desired environment/culture. Consider:
     - Physical organization
     - Forms of engagement
     - Daily lesson structure
   - Outlining a plan for how to enact each component. Include how students can practice the routine and how long it will take.

> Get an Early Start Thinking about and Establishing Routines!
>
> "I want to spend my teaching time teaching, so before the first day of school, I invite students and their families to come in and see the classroom. They bring their supplies, check out the room, and take a picture with me. This gives me time to label everything and put it in place and kids come in calmer because they know what to expect. They aren't rattled. They know where everything is."
>
> —*Jenn*

3. *Break Down Which Routines Are Procedural, Organizational, and/or Pedagogical*—To determine the best place and method of integrating each routine into your classroom experience:
   - Categorize your routines. Examples include:
     - *Procedural*—Starting/ending an activity, transitions, lining up, quieting down, hand signals for agreement/questions/asking for help, leaving the classroom
     - *Organizational*—Cleaning up stations/supplies, where to turn in work
     - *Pedagogical*—Working with partners/groups, engaging in class discussions, using technology
   - Plan (within your lesson plans) when and how to introduce, model, and practice each routine.

> "Everything I do is premeditated. Everything is laid out so things are smooth."
> —*Jenn*

4. *Integrate Routines into Plans for First Days of School*—Make sure you find space in your schedule during the first few days of the school year to integrate and practice each routine. Determine:
   - How many new routines you can realistically and productively introduce each day.
   - The order in which you want to introduce each routine.
   - Where in your lesson you want to integrate each routine.
   - How often you want to reinforce each routine.
   - Which routines you can wait to integrate until after the first week of school.

5. *Discuss, Assess, and Collaboratively Agree upon Routines with the Class*—While you already determined the routines you would like to integrate into your class, when you would like to integrate them, and how you would like to integrate them, once you meet your class, it is helpful to make them partners in the roll out of each routine. To do this:
   - Be transparent with your students about the overall environment you want to create. Ask students to contribute ideas for how they might add onto or change that overall environment.
   - Brainstorm routines that will support the type of environment the class wants.
   - Discuss each routine and get feedback from the class about: how well it will work, what it will take to consistently work, and if there is anything they would change about it.
   - Record the components of each routine (on paper and digitally if you can) as an anchor that students can reference after the roll out of each routine.
   - Ask students to add routines and go through the same process.

6. *Practice Routines*—Based on the order you decided to roll out the routines:
   - Introduce one routine at a time.

- Practice the routine as many times as needed to ensure students understand and buy into it.
- Continue to enact the routine daily, practicing it each new day until it becomes second nature for the class.

7. *Reassess Routines and Adapt as Needed*—If you notice a routine is no longer working as you and the class intended, take time to reassess.
   - Engage your class in a *Plus/Delta* discussion about what is working well with the routine and what you could change to strengthen it. (See *Failing Forward Strategy in Action* on page 32.)
   - Periodically reassess all routines even if they seem to be working.
   - Consider new routines that would help your class achieve its desired environment.
   - Repeat Steps 5 and 6 for any changed or new routine.

CONSIDERING DIFFERENT TYPES OF LEARNERS

Establishing Routines can be adapted for different types of learners:

1. *English Language Learners* benefit from routines that do not rely exclusively on English instructions; rather, utilize routines that emphasize symbols, hand gestures, and signals.
2. Routines are often particularly useful for *Special Education* students. Try to create routines that align with the special education students' 504 plans and Individual Education Plans (IEPs).

How to Implement the Strategy at Varied Grade Levels

Elementary	*Middle*	*High*
*Work in collaboration with families/guardians outside of school to create a welcoming classroom environment and reinforce routines. *Lots of practice with routines, making the first couple weeks of school focused more on routine and environment building than curricular content. *Make routines silly and fun when appropriate.	*Work with both families/ guardians and directly with the students (email, remind.com, etc.) to create, reinforce, and maintain the classroom environment and routines. * Make the first week of school focused more on routine and environment building than curricular content. *Keep routines silly and fun when appropriate.	*Communicate with students directly outside of school (e.g., email, remind.com, etc.) *Stress and practice routines during the first week and revisit them, but you can focus on content while reinforcing routines. *You can make routines silly and fun, but they will more often be about function.

STRATEGY IN ACTION: ESTABLISHING ROUTINES BY USING BASE GROUPS

"*Setting up base groups:* I have students submit requests with five students they want to work with and an option to veto one student they know they absolutely cannot work together with (most don't use their veto). I put the groups together and guarantee they will be with one person they requested.

Example:

YOUR NAME

1)	4)
2)	5)
3)	VETO:

Teaching cooperative learning skills: It's really important to explicitly teach students how to work together instead of just hoping they figure it out. I use a handout to teach cooperative learning skills. The two main resources I use and to teach my students are Baloche, *The Cooperative Classroom: Empowering Learning* and Tuckman's *Stages of Group Development*. Periodically, I have students assess how well their groups are functioning together according to that handout. These cooperative learning check-ins are also a good time to set goals for how groups can improve themselves.

What to do with your groups: Create icebreakers, activities, jigsaws, discussions, evaluations, assignments, presentations, and assessments for your base groups so that the group becomes important for them.

Roles within base groups: For almost all activities, assign roles within groups so each group member has something they are responsible for. Also, switch up the roles and specialize them for each activity so not everyone is the same role every time. Roles I commonly use are: Discussion Leader, Recorder, Reporter, Timekeeper, Taskmaster, Group Leader, Content Expert, Research Director, Graphic Designer, Presenter, Presentation Director, Reader, Artist, Group Representative. After I ask them to choose roles, I then have all the 'Discussion Leaders, etc.' raise their hands, so that I know they actually have roles.

Troubleshooting: Not all groups will reach the stage of 'performing.' Some groups might end up dysfunctional, some will get into fights, and some may encounter other obstacles. Obstacles are normal. It's important to have the groups work through challenges so they learn to overcome conflicts and issues. Oftentimes, problems solve themselves as the groups realize they will be working together for the long haul and need to work through their differences."

—*Beth Merrill*

Adaptation for Different Assets/Needs

Class Size	
Small Class	*Large Class*
*Embrace collaboratively establishing routines so each student feels like they are playing a major role in creating and maintaining the routines.	*Understand you will likely need to practice and reinforce each routine more than in smaller classes until you have as close to 100% buy-in as possible. *Assign "Routine Leaders" in the class so they can help you lead and reinforce routines.
Cultural Diversity	
Limited Diversity	*Lots of Diversity*
*Create routines that align with the cultural norms and backgrounds of the student population (e.g., Call and Response, particular hand gestures, ways to communicate with one another, etc.) *Create some routines that align to dominant cultural norms and explicitly discuss why you are doing the routines and how this can support students with *code switching*.	*Learn about the cultural norms and backgrounds of your students. *Create routines that are representative of all of your students, highlighting how certain routines align with certain cultural backgrounds. This will also help students learn about one another's cultures in a positive way.

STRATEGY IN ACTION: GETTING STUDENTS TO FEEL COMFORTABLE IN YOUR CLASSROOM BEFORE DAY 1

"To start the year off right for my Kindergarten class, I take the following steps:

1. Find out the district designated day for families to drop-off supplies in the classroom.
2. Send a letter telling parents that I will be there that day and inviting them to bring their Kindergarteners with them so they can meet me and see their classroom.
3. Set up my classroom early so that it is ready for parents and students to see when they come with supplies. Make sure to:
   a. Label spaces in the classroom (e.g., Literacy Centers, extra handouts, art supplies)
   b. Create and label filing systems that are accessible and easy to understand
   c. Have an open classroom layout that is easy for students to navigate
   d. Make resources easily accessible
   e. Offer alternative seating options (if possible)
4. On supply drop-off day, have snacks ready so it feels like a party.
5. Students bring supplies and find their spaces (cubbies, seats at tables, library, stations)
6. Take selfies together.
7. Once I have all the supplies, I label them and get them in place *before* Day 1 of school."

—*Jenn*

WHY I LIKE THIS STRATEGY

"I really want kids to feel safe and secure and to feel like somebody is putting a lot of effort for them so they put forth that effort back. When things are in place and they are not spending time worrying about what is to come, it helps kids. Kids tend to act out in order to get some control when they don't feel control. If I can help them feel some control over their environment and know what is happening, they are a little bit more in control of their emotions."

—Jenn

STRATEGY 3: POSITIVE AFFIRMATIONS

Chapter Contributors
Caitlin Cahill, PS 503 (NY), Kindergarten and 5th grade
Chad Frade, Urban Assembly Maker HS (NY), 9th–12th grade

Positive affirmations is a strategy designed to recognize the behavioral and/or academic accomplishments of students either publicly or privately using compliments and gestures, which helps create an environment where students feel welcomed, appreciated, and respected. Different types of affirmations (e.g., claps, cheers, high fives, chants, etc.) may be taught by the teacher or created by the students themselves. Students who are awarded a positive affirmation may be invited to select their favorite affirmation, making it an especially encouraging acknowledgment. This strategy can support students in taking academic risks because they will feel supported rather than judged.

STRATEGY IMPLEMENTATION

1. *Greet Students at the Door*—As students enter your room, greet them with a positive or welcoming tone—small moments for genuine interactions (e.g., "Did you see the game?"; "I love those sneakers"; or "I thought of you when I heard this Drake song."). During this time, you can also direct students to what they should be doing for the start of class. Remember to:
   - Pay attention to each student's affect.
   - Individually address something positive and welcoming about each student before they enter the room.
   - Set the day's expectations for students when they enter the room.

2. *Starting Class*—Thank students for being part of the class. If someone comes late, tell them "This class is not complete without you." Let students know the day's expectations for success and reinforce that they are fully capable of accomplishing whatever task/activity you have for them.

Establishing Positive Affirmations as Part of Group Norms

- During the first week of school, *with students*, create a list of behaviors or habits that can earn affirmations. Examples include (but are not limited to), being:
  - prepared with materials
  - an active listener
  - respectful (of space, not talking while others are talking, making eye contact with a speaker)
  - a good partner/helper
- Practice the norms created by the class. Affirm students when they carry out these norms.
- Continue to revisit, revise as necessary, and reinforce the positive affirmations throughout the year.
- Post the affirmations in your classroom. If you "retire" some affirmations or create new ones, post the new list.

3. *Use Positive Affirmations during Whole Class or Small Group Instruction*—When engaging in whole class or small group instruction, find multiple ways to give positive affirmations. The goal is to give positive affirmations to each student multiple times per week.

   Teacher-to-Student—When you as the teacher want to "gift" an affirmation to a student or students (either individually or in front of the class), make sure you:
   - Give positive affirmations to a variety of students.
   - Consider what behavior/action/product you want to affirm.
   - Figure out what kind of positive affirmation you want to give the student (see options below).
   - Determine whether the affirmation will be whole class or more subtle.
   - Think about how you are integrating the affirmation(s) into your instruction (stopping instruction or within the flow of instruction).

   > Remember!
   >
   > "Positive Affirmations shouldn't be linked to compliance. . . . It should not be a mode to control students. Instead give students strategies on how to think and then assess based on that. . . . This is what you praise!"
   >
   > —*Chad Frade*

   Whole Class—When the entire class collectively acknowledges something great a student or students have done. The teacher will ask students what kind of cheer they want and then count down "3, 2, 1," then do it together. Think about:
   - When the whole class should do an affirmation as opposed to just the teacher.
   - Who in the class determines which student gets the whole class affirmation.
   - Whether the student being affirmed gets to choose their affirmation or the person who decided to "gift" the affirmation gets to.
   - If more than one student should be acknowledged at a time.
   - How the affirmations are integrated into the instruction.

   Student-to-Student—When students shout out something great one of their peers has done. Consider:

   - If students are able to offer affirmations whenever they want during class or only during designated times.
   - Whether there is a limit to how many students can offer affirmations at one time.
   - When student-to-student affirmations can turn into whole class affirmations.

4. *Using Positive Affirmations during Independent or Pair Work*—When students are doing independent or pair work, take time to check in on each student and offer affirmations to support their work and spirit. Decide whether:
   - Particular students really need a "pick me up" today.

- You keep the affirmation between you and the student/pair or open it up to the whole class.

5. *Student Choice in Affirmation*—If not using Teacher-to-Student verbal affirmations, consider letting students know you want to give them an affirmation for "X" action and to select how they would like to be positively affirmed for it. Decide when the student:
   - Selects from *pre-existing* class affirmations.
   - *Creates their own* affirmation.

Get to Know Your Students

"You just really need to get to know your students and their interests when coming up with the best and most effective positive affirmations! This makes students feel special, heard, and recognized when the affirmation aligns with their interests."

—*Caitlin Cahill*

"Positive affirmation is based on how you build your relationship with your students. . . . If students know they are appreciated and valued, they are more likely to put forth the effort."

—*Chad Frade*

Sample Affirmations

- Claps
  - Roller Coaster clap (hands going up and down like a roller coaster)
  - Fireworks clap (clap with hands going all over the place like fireworks exploding)
  - Spiderman clap (shoot webs at each other)
  - Quiet (not verbal)
  - Snaps
  - Rubbing hands together
  - ASL Silent applause (waving both hands back and forth)
- Verbal
  - Come up with a phrase or song lyric that captures the affirmation
  - Simply state what you liked about what the person did

NOTE from Caitlin Cahill: Affirmations get more creative as the year goes on. Students get to align affirmations with their interests, which is often aligned to content as well! (e.g., When learning about big blue whales, students created a "whale clap" in a whale voice.)

CONSIDERING DIFFERENT TYPES OF LEARNERS

Positive Affirmations can be adapted for different types of learners:

1. *English Language Learners and Special Education* students (and likely some other nonclassified students) might be intimidated or nervous about affirmation choice or they might not like to be the center of attention. Therefore, you could have a jar where they pick a random affirmation to take the pressure off making

that choice. Start by asking the student if they want to choose an affirmation or if you can recognize them in a different way.

2. Also, for *students who struggle with self-esteem*, recognize that praise exists in spaces with some errors (see Strategy 4: Failing Forward). Praise students for their positive attempts and the risks they take, then after the affirmation, focus on the feedback used to refine the attempt. Be really explicit and clear with feedback.

STRATEGY IN ACTION: POSITIVE AFFIRMATIONS BUILD CLASSROOM COMMUNITY

"I used to teach a stand-alone English as a New Language (ENL) kindergarten class in which I regularly used positive affirmations, especially when students modeled math strategies on the rekenrek [Abacus] in front of the whole class. Since my students were still learning English, positive affirmations was a strategy I used to push them to speak publicly in strong voices. Each time a nervous student modeled their strategy we celebrated by giving them a positive affirmation of their choice. Many students began by picking from our regular list of affirmations (firework clap, rollercoaster clap, etc.) but gradually students began to expand to other cheers that they created themselves. I remember one day, a particularly shy student came to the rekenrek and was too shy to show the work that he had done. Another student suggested that we give him a cheer. I asked him, 'What cheer would you like us to give you?' to which he replied, 'Pizza.' 'Pizza' was not a cheer that we knew yet, so I asked him how it went. He lit up and showed us how to move our fingers and say 'pizza' just the right way. We all did it in unison and then he felt comfortable enough to show his work. That same student went on to invent the 'It's me, Mario!' clap which became a class favorite. Positive affirmation helped me to build a strong classroom community because students felt comfortable taking risks knowing that their friends were there to support them."

—*Caitlin Cahill*

How to Implement the Strategy at Varied Grade Levels

Elementary	*Middle*	*High*
*Make it silly and fun. *Focus more on behaviors and actions. *Be strategic about using affirmations after any partner or group work and at the end of the lesson. *When students are in independent work, keep track of those who struggle and then celebrate them more regularly to inspire more on-task behavior in the future.	*Make positive affirmations around sophisticated thinking. Take the time to support and discuss their thinking and learning. *Allow students to "fail," but support what they did and give individual encouragement to move forward. Praise the attempt and then support them. *Create a climate where it's OK to be silly.	*Embed affirmations more into the content. *Develop a climate where student-to-student affirmations become more commonplace. *Allow for student choice where they can create what they deem to be age-appropriate affirmations (e.g., song lyrics, name of artist they like, weird meme, etc.).

WHY I LIKE THIS STRATEGY

"I like using this strategy because it feels very natural and fits easily into my practice. It is a way to acknowledge positive behaviors, make a big deal about them, and then get back on track. I also like how active chants, cheers, and claps can be. Unfortunately, classroom life can be quite sedentary. Positive affirmations are another way to get students moving and get their blood flowing. Additionally, positive affirmations are a great way to foster classroom community. Involving students in praising each other, and inviting them into the process of creating 'creative' praise is a fun way to have students collaborate with one another."

—*Caitlin Cahill*

"When students feel welcomed, appreciated, respected, and that someone believes in them, they will take the academic risks that we will ask them to try. Positivity (or 'positive energy' as students will say that you have) enables students to feel that they have an ally. Additionally, it requires that you highlight the positive happening in your class (deficit-based thinking is prevalent, especially when teachers may feel that they don't have control over the class). The positive affirmations work when you know what you want students to do and then you can be on the lookout for students who are modeling the behaviors and student-moves you want to see."

—*Chad Frade*

Modify Positive Affirmations for Students' Personalities and Cultural Backgrounds!

"Positive Affirmations can be modified to match any personality (teacher or student) and the message that is given."

—*Chad Frade*

"Cultural differences in the classroom won't impact the use of Positive Affirmations. The affirmations they generate and individual student interests might be different, but the process remains the same . . . though, you could do celebrations in other languages."

—*Caitlin Cahill*

Adaptation for Different Assets/Needs

Class Size	
Small Class	*Large Class*
*Smaller classes can create more intimacy, but also students are more visible. Find ways to make the affirmations aligned with the deeper relationships while respecting that sometimes students need space. *You can listen a lot more; therefore, take the time to hear what your students have to say before and after doing affirmations. *Try to give one positive affirmation for each student every day.	*Larger classes are more spontaneous and you don't know who is going to be the day's superstar. *Try to give each student positive affirmations at least twice a week (rather than three or four times a week). *Embrace the energy of the large class and use that for the whole class affirmations. *Be mindful that you spread out the affirmations. With larger classes, it is harder to keep track of it. Use a method (tally chart, popsicle sticks, etc.) to keep track of which students you have given affirmations to throughout the day and to help determine who you should acknowledge later in the day or tomorrow.
Teacher Personality	
Reserved/Strict	*Outgoing/Humorous*
*Do more subdued affirmations. *Select a student (could be on a rotating basis) to be the "Affirmations Coach." That student can then lead the class on the teacher's request. *Assign an "Affirmations Spotter" to "spot" behaviors/actions/products that are deserving of affirmations. *Use stamps or other nonverbal ways to show the students they are doing something great.	*Create a classroom culture where affirmations can be as silly and fun(ny) as possible. *Model as many affirmations as you can, using your voice, your body, and your energy. *Use affirmations as a way to support more reserved students becoming comfortable being celebrated.

Look Out for Your Students

"They know that if they fail, either: a) I will be there to help them fix it; or b) I'll find something that they did in the attempt that will help them be successful."

—*Chad Frade*

STRATEGY IN ACTION: THE IMPACT OF POSITIVE AFFIRMATION

"This year, my senior English class was rough. Routinely, they were angry at me for demanding what they called 'too much work.' They were upset that we were reading Zora Neale Hurston's *Their Eyes Were Watching God* because of her use of the vernacular. One student in particular, Victor, a Latino male with an IEP who had anger issues, said that my class was too hard. However, Victor arrived routinely to my 2nd period class with 10–15 minutes left of class. Every time Victor entered the class, I greeted Victor with a smile, told him 'Good Morning!' and told him what the expectation was for the task. When Victor would get angry because he was confused by the work or did not understand what he was supposed to do, I would crouch down, focusing on my tone and my volume, and in a calm, caring, and intentionally whispery manner, I would repeat the expectations/directions, direct him to a student exemplar or a student who could help him, and then say, 'I know that this is hard and that it might be confusing, but I do believe that you can accomplish this task. I appreciate that you are trying, and here is what I need you to do. . . .'

Sometimes Victor would storm out, but most of the time (about 80% of the time), because of my calm and positive demeanor, he would cooperate. It wasn't a power struggle; I had to work to not be sarcastic or at all frustrated because he would shut down when I observed him with other teachers, so I eventually got him to write something, and while not perfect, he did attempt the work, and in doing so, I could give him feedback and let him know how to improve the work. I praised him for trying and in doing that he was able to engage.

I needed to be able to assess Victor's work, and because I chose to highlight that he had not left the class in frustration, I could leverage the fact that my tone and demeanor were keeping him there. Eventually, after some time and a couple of parent-phone calls, he started to engage with the work, and while he complained a great deal, he wrote a 7–10 page paper on Hurston's novel. I supported him and he knew that on Mondays at our school's writing center, that I would be there and I could help him. By the end of the year, Victor needed some extra supports to finish the year; he said to me that he was relieved that I was the person helping him because I never got mad at him and he believed that I believed in him."

—*Chad Frade*

STRATEGY 4: FAILING FORWARD

Chapter Contributors
Christine Mercer, Yardville Elementary School (NJ), 4th grade
Kaity Haley, Grover Middles School (NJ), 8th grade

Failing Forward means looking at mistakes, poor decisions, or not being where we want to be as learners, in order to grow from what has happened. Students and teachers alike are encouraged to share their shortcomings and recognize that though they may have failed, they themselves are not failures. This approach is highly reflective and grounded in social-emotional learning. It encourages students to recognize their own failures, take pride in them as a part of the learning process, and make decisions about what to do next.

STRATEGY IMPLEMENTATION

1. *Create a Safe, Shared Environment*—Help students feel comfortable sharing their failures by:
   - Sharing videos or stories of successful people who have failed many times on their path to success.
   - Sharing your own failure with the class.
   - Offering a variety of brain teasers and challenges designed for students to fail a few times before they find success. You can choose whether to be explicit with students in explaining that they are likely to struggle and/or fail, or you can let them experience this without forewarning.

> Tips for Creating a Comfortable Space
>
> Some students may not feel comfortable sharing or experiencing their failure. You may want to gauge students' comfort levels by asking:
>
> - To what degree are you comfortable facing/talking about failure?
> - How do you stay resilient and persistent in the face of failure?
> - Do you know of a time when someone in your family failed? How did people respond?

2. *Explain/Review Growth Mindset*—Let students know that their brains are wired to improve by:
   - Using a growth mindset self-assessment. See Figure 1.4.
   - Charting results of the self-assessment so students can see where there are commonalities in their responses and, noting that in most cases, people are a mix of fixed and growth mindset.
   - Watching a video or reading an article about growth mindset.
   - Having students develop a list of phrases/ways of thinking that reflect fixed and growth mindsets. (e.g., Fixed—"I can't do this"; Growth—"I need to work on my _____ skills to do this.")

3. *Encourage Reflection*—Reflection is not judgmental or punitive. This is a time for students to learn from mistakes and be proud of their efforts.

Possible Formats for Reflection:

- Teacher has a short conference with each student to ask questions and comment on reflections
- Small group share
- Full class share (see Failure Party narrative below)
- Journaling
- Drawing

Topics for Reflection:

- Specific skills to develop to be successful
- People who may help develop these skills
- Additional knowledge needed
- Where to go to find that information
- Level of motivation to complete the work
- What sparks motivation

A Note about Motivation

Motivation comes from the word "motive" which means the desire to satisfy a need. Often, in school, students are working to meet needs or goals set by the teacher or curriculum in order to earn a grade or praise (extrinsic motivation). Students will become lifelong learners when they are working to meet a need or desire for pride in their efforts or to satisfy their curiosity (intrinsic motivation).

CONSIDERING DIFFERENT TYPES OF LEARNERS

Failing Forward can be adapted for different types of learners:

1. *English Language Learners* might work on this in their native language because the goal is introspection. They could then translate part or all of their work to share.
2. *Special Education* students may benefit from scaffolding that includes sentence starters and/or a list of options for next steps.
3. *Gifted and Talented* students may feel uncomfortable sharing failures because they are used to being praised for their successes at school. It is important to stress the value of being able to use reflective/metacognitive skills to help them learn from failure.

STRATEGY IN ACTION: SOCIAL-EMOTIONAL FOUNDATIONS FOR FAILING FORWARD

"We begin each week with explicit instruction in Social Emotional Learning (SEL). This may include mindfulness or growth mindset strategies, learning about the brain, or goal setting. Each Friday, students are asked to reflect on how they used what they learned throughout the week. Students conference with me and reflect on ways they can improve and set a goal for the next week.

Working on SEL strengthens teacher-student relationships, and this enables students to be comfortable struggling with material and learning to deeply understand. It's OK not to be right all of the time. Students understand that we are more focused on the process. This allows them to have deeper discussions and make connections. They don't just understand on the surface, but much deeper. This safety gives students opportunities to explore further rather than just trying to finish something and find the 'right' answer.

—*Christine Mercer*

How to Implement the Strategy at Varied Grade Levels

Elementary	*Middle*	*High*
*Explicitly teach coping mechanisms such as deep breathing and taking a 10-second break to help students know what to do when they become frustrated. *Students can draw a picture of failure and what comes next. This will help to ensure that students are individually reflecting prior to sharing.	*Get student buy-in by having them help develop reflection questions/prompts for failing forward. *Collaborate with students to develop a list of next steps that students can take. This will remind them of the power they have to succeed!	*Consider ways to make this process more private. It could be done in small groups or posted anonymously online or on a bulletin board.

WHY I LIKE THIS STRATEGY

"It gives students an opportunity to think about their choices and how those choices made them feel. They are learning from these life experiences to make better informed decisions in the future."

—*Christine Mercer*

"Failing forward reminds students that a single failure is not the end of the world. It allows them the time and space to recognize the wrong choices they may have made, big or small, and learn lessons from them."

—*Kaity Haley*

Adaptation for Different Assets/Needs

Time	
Limited Time	*Lots of Time*
*Failure parties may be a good way to help students think about how failure helps them learn and how to move forward from it. This can take one class period or 40 minutes one or two times a year.	*Embed reflections on failing forward weekly. *Hold conferences with students to share their failures and what they learned. *Invite family, community members, and colleagues to share stories of failure and growth with the class.
Technology	
Low Tech	*High Tech*
*Create growth mindset surveys and/or reflection forms on 8×10 paper for students to complete individually, or use large-scale poster paper where students can respond to close-ended questions by placing stickers next to their answers. This creates a classroom visual that can be analyzed and discussed to make a plan for growth.	*Utilize Google Forms or an equivalent survey tool that is built to integrate diverse question types while also automatically recording answers in spreadsheets and tables. *Create a class blog or website to showcase failing forward.

STRATEGY IN ACTION: A FAILURE PARTY

"The first failure party I had was during my first full-year teaching. My students and I were exhausted heading into the holiday, and as a young teacher, I was beating myself up for some of the flops I had experienced that fall. When my students returned from break, they did not come back refreshed as I had hoped, and neither had I. So in an effort to remind them of their growth since September, I developed the failure party. We used it as a chance to laugh about all the mistakes we had made in the first semester, and students had the opportunity to realize that they had many of their failures in common with others. I was so excited to see the reaction of the rest of the students and staff, when my kids explained why they were wearing words on their necks in the hallway, especially when those words were often negative (e.g., disorganized, easily frustrated, forgetful). My students were able to explain their failures with pride, which shocked those around them."

—*Kaity Haley*

Sample Materials

DIRECTIONS: Circle the descriptor that best matches how much you agree with each of the following statements.

1. Intelligence is something that can change.
   Agree Somewhat Agree Disagree Strongly Disagree

2. I have the power to get smarter.
   Agree Somewhat Agree Disagree Strongly Disagree

3. Working hard makes me better at things.
   Agree Somewhat Agree Disagree Strongly Disagree

4. A perfect or high score on a test is the best way to show my ability.
   Agree Somewhat Agree Disagree Strongly Disagree

5. The quicker I get an answer, the smarter I am.
   Agree Somewhat Agree Disagree Strongly Disagree

6. When learning is easy for me, it means that I am smart.
   Agree Somewhat Agree Disagree Strongly Disagree

7. I can learn from my mistakes.
   Agree Somewhat Agree Disagree Strongly Disagree

Figure 1.4 Growth Mindset Survey. *Source*: Author created.

STRATEGY 5: CRITICAL FEEDBACK SURVEYS

Chapter Contributors
Kaity Haley, Thomas Grover Middle School (NJ), 8th grade
Brittany Klimowicz, NYC iSchool (NY), 9th–12th grade

Critical Feedback Surveys are focused, digital, and/or written surveys given to students to elicit feedback on specific learning activities, assessment, and/or other classroom experiences. Surveys can focus on the students' perceived success of various lesson strategies as well as the overall classroom climate, especially as it relates to each unit. Students are also asked to suggest or create action steps to make improvements to their own learning, an instructional activity, or the classroom environment. Teachers then integrate relevant student feedback into their future planning and practice, demonstrating a commitment to their students' thoughts and needs.

STRATEGY IMPLEMENTATION

1. *Purpose of the Survey*—Teacher and/or students identify what elements of their units/lessons/activities/classroom climate they want to critically reflect on and the scope of the intended feedback. Consider the following questions to guide your development of feedback surveys:
    - What elements of the units/lessons/activities/classroom climate can be strengthened by student feedback?
    - Do you need feedback related to how you implemented your learning experiences, the design of those experiences, or both?
    - Is the feedback for short- or long-term change?
2. *Type of Survey*—Based on the determined purpose of your survey, decide the type of survey you want to create to help you and your students meet the intended purpose. Think about:

> Getting Students to Buy into Using Critical Feedback Surveys
>
> - Start small, with brief surveys.
> - Implement the changes students suggest after every feedback survey from the start of the year.
> - Let students explicitly know how you are implementing their suggestions and why you are implementing them.
> - Be honest about why you are not integrating particular feedback from the students.
>
> "If you want them to be honest, they have to be able to be honest."
> —*Kaity Haley*

Survey Mode*:*

- Easiest mode of feedback (digital, written, or oral) for your students to complete
- Easiest mode of feedback for you and your students to analyze
- Technologies that can enhance the survey experience and product (e.g., Google Forms)
- Mode of feedback that will help students develop critical thinking skills

- Varying the mode of critical feedback surveys throughout the year to provide students multiple avenues to critically reflect on their classroom experiences/environment
- Time needed to analyze student feedback; digital or written feedback would allow for teachers and/or students to have more time to examine and analyze feedback
- *If oral*, consider:
  - The best way to ask the survey questions
  - How you will record student answers
  - Whether it will be done as a whole class, in small groups, or as a "turn and talk"

Reflective vs. Action-Oriented:

- If reflective, develop questions that will help students *look back* and critically reflect on topics like: where they struggled and excelled, the type of support they need, and how the classroom environment could be improved.
- If action-oriented, develop questions that will help students *look forward* and critically think about where and how they and their classroom community can grow and move forward.

3. *Survey Questions*—Figure out which question types align with your desired survey outcomes.
   - *Open-ended:* Used to elicit detailed, subjective information from students
   - *Likert:* Used to assess a range of feelings from least to most (e.g., How likely are you to use a graphic organizer like this again? Not likely, Somewhat likely, Very likely)
   - *Multiple Choice or Rankings:* Used when you want students to highlight or order their beliefs around a particular question
   - *Select All That Apply:* Used to give students choices to provide feedback within a contained number of selections

4. *Time Allocation for Survey*—Determine how much time is needed for students to complete the survey and when you can allocate that amount of time during class. Below are possible times you might want to have students complete the surveys:
   - Do informal check-ins with students after any learning experience to gauge their thoughts.
   - Have students complete *Exit Tickets* at the end of the lesson that ask them to critically reflect on particular elements of the day.
   - Give students a summative critical feedback survey at the conclusion of a project or unit.
   - Have students fill out a survey at the end of your marking period (or year).

Anonymity of Surveys

- Student anonymity is important for students to feel comfortable with sharing honestly.
- Give students the option of including their name if they want to identify themselves for a particular reason.
- If student anonymity is critical, shy away from written surveys because most teachers learn students' handwriting early in the year; therefore, anonymity is challenging.

5. *Analyze Student Feedback*—Analyze and make meaning of the feedback to prepare for your student debrief and begin to consider ways to implement the suggestions. Decide:
   - The best way to analyze the student feedback (e.g., take notes, make a list, write questions, etc.).
   - How you will make meaning of the student feedback.
   - How to debrief your analysis of the student feedback with your students.

6. *Debrief Feedback with Students*—Find the best time during your class period to debrief the feedback with your students. Ensure you allocate enough time so students feel heard and the debrief is collaborative rather than teacher-centered. To do this, consider:
   - The best time to have the debrief with the students (i.e., directly after receiving the feedback or at a later time).
   - How the discussion can be structured to support student voice.
   - How you will respond to student suggestions to ensure students feel heard.
   - Being transparent about how you plan to integrate their feedback (or not).
   - Preparing to have "tough conversations" with students about issues raised from the survey.

7. *Integrate Feedback into Your Teaching*—Try out the students' suggestions and be transparent about how and when you are implementing them.

8. *Reflect on Integration of Feedback*—Do your own critical reflection on the new changes and consider getting another round of student feedback on the effectiveness of the changes.

> "Using Critical Feedback Surveys makes students feel valued and that their opinions are important to you. If they see you as a partner in learning, they are OK with you pushing them. That relationship is important and once they buy-in, they will let you push them because they see you as someone who cares about them and wants them to succeed. Students feel special when you let them know you're trying something out and being honest with them. They appreciate when their thoughts are respected and honored."
>
> —*Brittany Klimowicz*

CONSIDERING DIFFERENT TYPES OF LEARNERS

Critical Feedback surveys can be adapted for different types of learners:

1. When working with *English Language Learners* (ELLs), remember that in many cultures the way that feedback is given and received varies. Do your best to: normalize giving constructive feedback with practice feedback surveys, model how a person might give constructive feedback, let students know that constructive feedback is helpful toward building a stronger classroom climate, and use humor

to break down barriers. Teachers can also adapt their surveys for ELLs to include sentence starters; letting questions be more surface level, and then support students getting to the next step; and giving options and support.

2. *Special Education* students would also benefit from scaffolding that includes sentence starters; letting questions be more surface level, and then supporting students getting to the next step; and giving options and support.
3. *Gifted and Talented* students often benefit from more metacognitive analysis in the survey as well as the development of concrete action plans.

STRATEGY IN ACTION: ORAL CRITICAL FEEDBACK

Oral Critical feedback can be in the form of a class "Plus/Delta" where students share elements of the learning experience they really like (Plus) and elements they want to change (Delta).

"I first heard about 'Plus/Delta' while attending a session on writing at the NJEA Teachers Convention. A 12*th* grade English teacher used it to give her students feedback. Thinking about the concept of Plus/Delta, I was curious how my students would react to it. I was teaching 6*th* grade and my students often struggled with providing specific feedback on the class. I always asked them for feedback on assessments, but they would leave simple phrases like 'it's good' or 'it was hard.' This did not give me anything to use as information for future lessons. I introduced Plus/Delta one day as a way to criticize my lesson. I knew it was one that students would struggle with. They first were asked for some positives, and then for some changes. I introduced the deltas by saying they could request any change, including the color of the walls or the marker I used to write on the board. This allowed them to enter the Plus/Delta discussion on a safe level. As the year progressed, I slowly pushed them for more specific changes, and then invited them to start considering their own Plus/Deltas. Peer feedback that had once happened using a checklist (that was honestly not very engaging) was now on a simple Plus/Delta chart. The feedback allowed for greater class discussions, as well as a practice in metacognitive skill that more 'traditional' feedback did not offer."

—*Kaity Haley*

"Critical feedback surveys have been a valuable tool to help me see what students valued, what seemed unnecessary, and what could be improved. It has helped me figure out how to make my courses stronger and cut through to the important parts of the curriculum for the next time I teach it."

—*Brittany Klimowicz*

How to Implement the Strategy at Varied Grade Levels

Elementary	*Middle*	*High*
*Use questions where students can choose emojis, circle answers, or draw pictures based on how they feel about the question. *Read the questions aloud. *Conference with students individually or in small groups to elicit feedback. *Most useful feedback will likely be about classroom culture/climate.	*Be very cognizant about how you introduce and use the survey. *Take extra care to start the year by creating a safe environment to share, discuss, and analyze critical feedback in supportive ways. *Begin to focus on metacognition.	*Be prepared to take more sophisticated and specific criticism from your students and turn that criticism into positive change for the class (without taking criticism personally). *Extend students' thinking about metacognition.

Adaptation for Different Assets/Needs

Technology	
Low Tech	*High Tech*
*Create surveys on paper or orally (though you cannot have anonymity if done orally).	*Utilize Google Forms or an equivalent survey tool that is built to integrate diverse question types while also automatically recording answers in spreadsheets and tables.
School Culture	
Not Part of School Culture	*Part of School Culture*
*Start small, be transparent, and focus more on your students than about the school environment. *Be honest with yourself and your students about what you want to change within the classroom and within the school. Then slowly work toward changing the culture within your own classroom. *Share how you use critical feedback surveys in your classroom with your colleagues/administrators and how it has had a positive impact. *Ensure students won't be punished for advocating for change outside of your classroom.	*Support your students in using their feedback surveys to effect positive change inside your classroom and within the larger school. *Work collaboratively with stakeholders in your school to support student efficacy.

WHY I LIKE THIS STRATEGY

"This strategy is the foundation of a classroom where all students feel valued. By not just asking for feedback, but then listening and determining action steps (Deltas) that can be taken by the teacher and/or students; everyone has agency."

—Kaity Haley

"By using this strategy, I get another perspective on my curriculum. As teachers we spend so much time in our own world of content that we sometimes forget what it's like for a learner approaching the material for the first time. It's always good to get a perspective from the very individuals (the students) you are engaging in the work."

—Brittany Klimowicz

STRATEGY IN ACTION: A SCHOOL AND CLASS-BASED APPROACH

"This is my second year at the NYC iSchool and it's a completely different world from where I used to work. At my new school we have block scheduling, project-based courses, classes with students of all grade levels, a school culture where students get to pick their own schedule, and almost 150 different courses that we offer to students including electives about Asian Trade, Astrobiology, Superhuman Physiology, and 'Pop-Up Restaurants.' The teachers at the iSchool are incredibly innovative and work extremely hard to provide students with one of the most unique experiences in high school. It's been an incredible learning experience for me as a teacher to see how vastly different two schools, only 50 blocks apart, can operate so differently. Part of the iSchool mission is '360-degree feedback.' This means, administration gives feedback to teachers, who give feedback to students, who give feedback to teachers, who give feedback to administration.

As a school we have a standard Google Form that gets sent to students at the end of each quarter. I found that while that information was interesting, it didn't always help me figure out specific fixes for the individual courses I was teaching, so I decided to make course-specific feedback forms. These forms helped me adapt my curriculum faster and with student-specific suggestions. Students have given great suggestions. For example, in my 'Happiness 101' elective students recommended that the weekly homework assignments have specific questions that are then talked about in class. That simple but specific suggestion helped me improve my homework and made it feel more useful and important for students."

—Brittany Klimowicz

Sample Materials

See the following survey used by Brittany Klimowicz as a guide for your surveys:

Shark Tank Module Feedback

Directions: Fill out this feedback form as honestly as possible as it will help us create a better course for future students.

1. On a scale of 1-10, how interesting did you find this module?

1 2 3 4 5 6 7 8 9 10

Not that interesting Really interesting!

2. On a scale of 1-10, how much did you learn during this module?

1 2 3 4 5 6 7 8 9 10

Didn't learn much Learned a lot!

3. What was your favorite activity we did during this module?

4. What was your least favorite activity we did during this module?

5. Would it have been better if the teacher chose the topic/problem that you worked on during this module instead of you choosing your own?
    - Yes
    - No
    - Maybe

6. What are some topics you wished we explored during this module?

7. If you had to create your own module, what would the topic be?

8. Anything else you would like us to know?

Figure 1.5 Sample Feedback Survey. *Source*: Brittany Klimowicz.

Chapter 2

Planning Strategies

This chapter explores the following approaches to planning:

- Developing a *Yearlong Overview* of unit progression based on Understanding by Design (UbD) (Strategy 6)
- Engaging in *Collaborative Planning* with colleagues within and among grade levels and content areas (Strategy 7)
- *Using Assessments to Guide Instruction* and individualize next steps based on students' needs (Strategy 8)
- Creating *Inquiry-Based Learning* experiences that engage students and further specific knowledge, skills, and dispositions (Strategy 9)
- Committing to *Culturally Responsive/Sustaining Teaching* that honors students' strengths and promotes an asset-based perspective (Strategy 10)

While Strategies 6–8 are focused on planning, Strategies 9 and 10 are hybrid strategies because they include additional information about planning implementation. Strategy 9 includes information on introducing, executing, assessing, and reflecting on the inquiry-based learning that you plan. Strategy 10 includes both how to gather information about your students and how to use that information to make your classroom and instruction more inclusive.

HELPFUL UNDERSTANDINGS

This chapter utilizes larger frames and ideas that you will see referenced often.

Using Understanding by Design (UbD)

UbD (also known as backward design/planning) has three main stages: desired results, assessment, and learning plan. This chapter examines how to use UbD to develop yearlong plans, units, and lessons that are cohesive and logical in helping students progress in their development of Knowledge/Skills/Dispositions (K/S/D).

Wiggins and McTighe (2004) make clear that this approach can be applied on a larger scale for curriculum mapping:

> Understanding by Design suggests a particular spin on the mapping process: Instead of simply listing the topics taught, a UbD map specifies the big ideas and essential questions that are addressed at various points in the curriculum. . . . Additionally, we propose that a UbD map should include core assessment tasks that all students would perform to demonstrate their understanding of key ideas and processes. (Of course, these tasks would be accompanied by agreed-upon scoring rubrics.) We believe that such curriculum mapping brings conceptual clarity and coherence to the curriculum. (p. 26)

In the strategies that follow in this chapter, you will read about large-scale planning for the year and for continued good planning practices throughout the year. You will also read about planning that can be smaller scale (e.g., inquiry projects and changes to unit plans to be more culturally responsive).

UbD Highlights

- See step-by-step guidance for including standards and assessments in your planning in *Yearlong Overview* (Strategy 6).
- Find advice for focusing on your purpose when working with others in *Collaborative Planning* (Strategy 7).
- Read *Using Assessments to Guide Instruction* (Strategy 8) to help you think deeply about what assessments will work best to help you and your students determine what students need.
- Explore *Inquiry-Based Learning* (Strategy 9) to learn how to determine a project's big ideas and link to essential questions, objectives, and evidence.
- Dive into *Culturally Responsive/Sustaining Teaching* (Strategy 10) and consider how to diversify and personalize learning that is grounded in meaningful desired results.

Planning for Differentiation and Scaffolding

This chapter discusses how to differentiate planning by considering students' interests, readiness, and learning modalities. Based on what is understood about students, the strategies that follow give guidance on how to adapt with appropriate content, process, and products that align with where students are and where you want them to go with their learning.

Scaffolding is when teachers provide support to students, as needed, and then gradually help students move toward working independent of teacher support. According to Great School Partnership's (2015) overview of scaffolding:

> The term itself offers the relevant descriptive metaphor: teachers provide successive levels of temporary support that help students reach higher levels of comprehension and

> skill acquisition that they would not be able to achieve without assistance. Like physical scaffolding, the supportive strategies are incrementally removed when they are no longer needed, and the teacher gradually shifts more responsibility over the learning process to the student. (https://www.edglossary.org/scaffolding/)

For all students, but in particular English Language Learners (ELLs), special education students, and students with low self-esteem (and other nonclassified students), it is important to focus on student assets and strengths and not deficits.

Differentiation and Scaffolding Highlights

- Check out the *Strategy in Action: Collaborative Reflection to Inform Planning* in *Collaborative Planning* (Strategy 7) to learn more about how one contributor worked weekly with colleagues to adapt instruction based on how students were progressing.
- Discover fun ways to use sticky notes to see what "stuck with" students and what needs reinforcing in new ways in *Using Assessments to Guide Instruction* (Strategy 8).
- Pay attention to *Instructions Three Ways* in *Inquiry-Based Learning* (Strategy 9). This is a good reminder that students may need multiple modes of communication (written on board, oral, individual page)
- Use *Culturally Responsive Teaching* (Strategy 10) to explore making connections with students' backgrounds/culture, creating an environment where every student is heard, and *Show and Tell*!

Maintaining Flexibility

Remember as you read through this planning chapter that *a flexible life is a happy life*. While this chapter encourages you to have a large-scale vision for classroom learning, it is important to maintain flexibility with this vision. Only make copies of, or post materials for instruction a few days in advance because you may need to make changes based on conversations in your classroom or skills that need further development. During a keynote address, Grant Wiggins, the designer of UbD, stated, "Plan . . . [dramatic pause] . . . to adapt." Wiggins himself made clear the importance of being open to change based on students' needs.

GUIDING QUESTIONS

As you read through this chapter, consider the following:

- How do I incorporate the UbD framework (desired results, assessment, learning plan) in my curriculum mapping and unit planning?
- In what ways can I contribute to collaborative planning? How will I benefit from this experience?

- How can I use assessment to inform my planning in ways that are meaningful for my students?
- How and when do students have a voice in their learning? What can I do to increase this voice when planning?
- In what ways can I differentiate/scaffold ahead of time for student success?
- What new and engaging strategies am I willing to try in my classroom? Why are these a good fit for my students?
- What can I do to incorporate more culturally responsive/sustaining teaching in my planning?

STRATEGY 6: YEARLONG OVERVIEW

Chapter Contributors
Kimberly Murray, Colegio Karl C. Parrish (Colombia), Kindergarten
Lindsay Davis, The Baldwin School (VA), 10th–12th grade

Creating a Yearlong Overview begins by using Understanding by Design (UbD) to align the year's larger learning objectives with the course's map. The overview breaks down how each course unit and lesson build toward achieving those yearlong goals and provides a basic structure and pacing guide for the year. This is a holistic view of the year that frames the way you develop your day-to-day lesson plans. The Yearlong Overview is not about writing every lesson plan months in advance of teaching; it is about developing a frame for outlining unit and lesson ideas that fit a larger vision of learning for the year.

STRATEGY IMPLEMENTATION

1. *Create a Yearlong Calendar/Template*—Create an academic year calendar template that includes all school days, school breaks, Professional Development (PD), school-wide activities, and any other event that will impact your instruction.
   - If available, use an already existing academic calendar template created by your school, district, or somewhere else.
   - Adapt the calendar template to make it accessible for you (e.g., change fonts, highlight, etc.).
   - Consider whether you want a digital or hard copy of the template, or both. If digital, add the calendar to a cloud-based system (Google Drive, Dropbox, etc.) so it is backed up.

When to Create Your Yearlong Overview
- It is typically helpful to begin creating your Yearlong Overview *a month before the school year begins* or once you have a solid academic calendar of school events, breaks, school closures, PDs, and so on.
- Build in time to *collaborate with colleagues* and align material before the school year starts.

2. *Get to Know Course Standards and Learning Objectives*—Identify and examine the relevant course standards (national and/or state) as well as any course-provided learning objectives (national, state, or district). You can use these standards and learning objectives to brainstorm themes for units that become frames for unit plans. Think about how you will:
   - Unpack the language of the standards and learning objectives to make them more accessible for you and your students, and to meet the needs of your students.
   - Address the skills and content needs of each student.
   - Ensure your students are able to meet these standards and objectives.
   - Determine which standards are complex and will require that you integrate supports to help your students meet the standards and objectives.

3. *Think Backwards*—Apply the three stages of UbD (desired results, assessment, and learning plan) to determine where you want students to end up at the end of the year and then how you will help them get there. Begin by thinking about the end-of-year goals and then how each unit goal will help build toward the end-of-year goals. Determine:
   - The larger enduring understandings and essential questions you want your students to take away from your class *by the end of the year.*
   - What enduring understandings and essential questions students will need to answer during your *units* in order to master the larger enduring understandings and essential questions for the year.
4. *Map Out Curricular Units*—Based on your analysis of standards and learning objectives (step 2) and the development of your desired results (step 3), determine what units are essential to teach your class during the year. Then, sequence the units on your calendar. Consider:
   - The most logical way to sequence your units to build toward the end-of-year goals.
   - Whether the sequencing of your units makes sense.
   - If the unit sequencing helps your students build their skills and content knowledge from one unit to the next.
5. *Add Assessments and Align to Standards*—Once the units are mapped out on your calendar, determine potential assessments to measure student mastery of each unit's enduring understandings, essential questions, skills, content, and/or dispositions. Make sure to:
   - Integrate both formative and summative unit assessments to align with standards and meet the big ideas for the unit and year.
   - Ensure your assessment sequencing throughout the year helps support skill and content development.
   - Create a diversity of traditional and nontraditional assessments to engage and assess your students.

   Note: While it is great to plan ahead, be ready to adapt your assessments as you get to know your students' strengths and needs.
6. *Add Daily Lesson Topics and Outline of Activities (Lesson Plan Outline)*—The final step in creating your initial Yearlong Overview is to fill in the lesson *topics* for each day of the year (within the context of each unit) and then *outline* the activities you want to include each day. Ensure:
   - Your lesson topics align with the big ideas for each unit and its summative assessment.
   - The sequencing of each lesson topic supports logical content and skill development.
   - Lesson activities are varied, engaging, and student-centered.

When to Add Details to Your Yearlong Overview
- Completely fill out the calendar outline for the first unit or two before school starts.
- Revisit the overview once you have met your students and adapt the calendar outlines for the first unit or two as necessary.
- Fill in the details of one unit at a time as the year goes on, at least a week before teaching it.

7. *Adapt Overview as Needed throughout the Year*—After the school year begins and you have met your students, it is important to revisit and update the Yearlong Overview to best support the learners in your classroom. Here are some tips on how to do so:
   - Fix something the minute you have to. If you don't get through something Monday, you fix the rest of the unit. Typically update it every few days.
   - Adjust the dates and schedule for your Yearlong Overview based on your students' needs, as you learn about new school events, curricular needs, and so on.
   - Make notations in red at the bottom of a page as a note for the next year.

STRATEGY IN ACTION: FIGURING OUT YEARLONG OVERVIEWS ON YOUR OWN

"I started this strategy when I was a second-year teacher at a new school, and my school did not have a lesson plan template or a place to send/upload my lesson plans. I am a very organized person who needs a plan in place. It is necessary for me to cover all of the needed material so that students can be successful in their next science class. So, without a set template, I created my own. After creating my pacing guide each year for each class, I share it unit by unit with my students on my website. This also allows them to be organized and plan ahead since they can see exactly what is coming up during a particular unit."

—*Lindsay Davis*

HOW THIS STRATEGY MIGHT BE ADAPTED BASED ON TEACHING EXPERIENCE

Early Career Teachers

Make sure you know your curriculum, what you want to teach, and how fast you have to go. Work with veteran teachers to better grasp pacing. Then try to figure out as much as you can about your students early in the year. Consider how they learn and what supports they need so you can adapt the overview as needed. Keep going back to veteran teachers (in your content area and in other areas) for advice and support.

Veteran Teachers

Be open to new approaches. Remember, each year, teaching looks different based on the students in your class, the community context in which you are teaching, the social context that students are understanding, and so much more!

WHY I LIKE THIS STRATEGY

"Planning is an essential part of the teaching process for me. I use backwards design to plan. This ensures that planning stays focused on learning objectives. Creating a YearLong Overview is very important for ensuring that all objectives are met and makes weekly/daily planning a lot easier."

—*Kimberly Murray*

Adaptation for Different Assets/Needs

Time Allocated for Teacher Prep	
Limited Time	*Lots of Time*
*Chunk by quarter or semester and plan one portion at a time. *Set aside more time before the school year begins to create the Yearlong Overview and fill in as many details as you can.	*Allocate one prep period per week (or every other week) that is dedicated to revisiting and revising the Yearlong Overview and associated unit and lesson plans.
Opportunities for Collaboration with Colleagues	
Limited Opportunities	*Lots of Opportunities*
*Rely on online teaching networks for feedback. (See *Strategy 17: Building and Supporting Your Professional Network* on page 112.) *Get feedback from students and administrators on your pacing and structure of the Yearlong Overview. *Set aside time each week during your prep time (in school or out of school) to revisit the Yearlong Overview and adapt as needed.	*With content area colleagues, talk about ensuring how everyone is on the same page in terms of getting through certain units within quarters while acknowledging you and your colleagues might have different approaches to teaching the content. *Have periodic check-ins with content area and grade-level colleagues to reevaluate your Yearlong Overview and discuss ways to best adapt it to meet the needs of your students.

STRATEGY IN ACTION: PLANNING A YEARLONG OVERVIEW WITH LOTS OF FREEDOM

"While working in a multi-age classroom in a nontraditional school, yearlong and lesson planning were challenging because I was given a lot of freedom. I had no curriculum and no requirements. I decided to use a mix of Common Core State Standards, Next Generation Science Standards, and Teaching Strategies Gold Standards as a guide. I tried to emphasize inquiry, play, and place-based philosophies. I tried to find a way to support the students in their own interests I observed in their play as well as in their questions. I tried to structure the day in a way to maximize their focus and concentration.

Eventually I created a schedule that worked for the students and me. This involved structuring the day with a combination of whole group vs. age/ability level groupings, structured vs. unstructured time with structured time including math, writing, and reading instruction, inquiry time guided by student interests, and unstructured time for play in nature and in the classroom. In order to ensure that student needs were met and students were supported in their progress toward increasingly complex learning and development goals, I created a lesson planning template to support the yearlong overview that reflected our daily schedule. This template made planning much easier, as I could insert learning activities into certain time slots during the day."

—*Kimberly Murray*

STRATEGY 7: COLLABORATIVE PLANNING

Chapter Contributors
Emilio Burgos, PS 360 (NY), 2nd Grade
Tina Tuminaro, Pond Road MS (NJ), 6th grade

Collaborative Planning can take place among teachers by grade level, subject, or teams of teachers who work with the same students. It can include a large group of teachers or as few as a pair of teachers. Some schools block time into teachers' schedules to allow for this collaboration while in other schools, teachers have to find their own time to coordinate with one another. When teachers meet to engage in collaborative planning, they may be reviewing assessment data, preparing curriculum/instruction, discussing social-emotional or behavioral needs of students, or developing ways to impact classroom, school, and/or community culture.

STRATEGY IMPLEMENTATION

1. *Find Your People*—You may be assigned to a group of colleagues as part of your Professional Development (PD) plan or nonteaching responsibilities. If not, or if you want an additional collaborative group, consider who is interested in collaborating. This may include groups based on grade level, common students, or common content. You can "sell" the idea of collaborative planning by noting the following benefits:
   - Improved morale due to support and feedback
   - Better teaching due to multiple perspectives and backgrounds
   - Insight into students' actions outside your classroom
   - Alignment among subjects and grade levels

> "Every school is talking about having students work collaboratively. Teachers need to do this too!"
> —*Emilio Burgos*

2. *Set Up a Time to Meet and Stick to It*—Collaborative planning may take place daily or, more likely, 2–3 times per week. To help you stick to the schedule you make, try the following:
   - Find a meeting place that is consistently available.
   - Send out an agenda with the meeting reminder email so people can prepare or consider ideas beforehand. This can be just one line (e.g., Discuss struggling students—bring names) or several items.
   - Invite administrators and support staff such as guidance counselors, social workers, and para-professionals. This will streamline their time in sharing information if they can talk to several teachers at once.

3. *Determine Roles*—Most collaborative planning teams are fairly casual. Think of a Professional Learning Community (PLC), but much more relaxed. That said, you may want to determine some key roles such as:

- Note-Taker/Note-Poster—Type up notes or revise materials and then post to a shared drive
- Scheduler—Email colleagues reminders of upcoming meetings
- Timekeeper—Just like students, teachers can get off track, so a timekeeper may be helpful in guiding groups back to their agenda

> "When it is too structured, the meeting cannot support natural collaboration."
> —*Tina Tuminaro*

4. *Focus on Your Purpose*—As a group, determine your purpose, and then connect back to it in the work you do. Remember, you might amend your original purpose and that is OK! You are evolving as a group. Determine:
   - What you want to do as a group
   - How your work will support students' development of Knowledge/Skills/Dispositions (K/S/D)
   - How your work will help the classroom, school, and/or larger community

> Ideas for Areas of Focus!
> - Mapping curriculum across grade levels/content areas
> - Selecting particular K/S/D and analyzing assessment data to inform instruction
> - Fostering school-home connections
> - Guiding at-risk students
> - Incorporating social-emotional learning

5. *Share Your Work*—When you work with a collaborative group, you push your thinking and expand your productivity. This is worth sharing with others! You might share your work with:
   - Other collaborative groups
   - Administrators
   - Colleagues at a faculty meeting or conference

STRATEGY IN ACTION: STARTING THE YEAR AS A TEAM

"It was the first day for teachers in my new school district. I was new to this particular school, but definitely not to teaching. Still, the nerves crept in, as they often do when meeting new people for the first time. As part of the school's professional development schedule, we were given a specific time and place to meet as a grade-level team. Immediately, I was put at ease as I was introduced to our team leader and a fantastic and caring team of teachers. We discussed the first days of school and the extended homeroom schedule. We discussed what we would need to accomplish, such as Chromebook distribution and locker assignments (with plenty of practice for first-time users—6th graders!). Teachers shared resources on Google Classroom with each other, such as documents of the students' daily schedules and a sheet for students to hang in their lockers with what they need for each class. At one point, the guidance counselor came in to give us pertinent information about some of the students we would teach this year. This strategy that my school implements throughout the year changes as needed. As a new teacher to the district, I was impressed by this strategy, as I've never quite seen this type of efficiency and dedication exhibited in this way."

—*Tina Tuminaro*

HOW THIS STRATEGY MIGHT BE ADAPTED BASED ON TEACHING EXPERIENCE

Early Career Teachers

Remember that you bring fresh eyes to your team. What might you see from a new perspective? What new skills, strategies, experience might you lend to next steps? Take initiative in asking to meet with colleagues. Visit their classrooms. Ask questions. This will bring greater dimension to your collaborative meetings.

Veteran Teachers

You have experience and institutional knowledge to share. Additionally, you will likely assume a mentor role for newer teachers. Consider getting mentor training. Remember that being a good teacher doesn't necessarily ensure that you will be a good mentor. Training can be helpful! Watch your mentees develop into veterans/mentors and carry on this process.

Adaptation for Different Assets/Needs

Timing	
Limited Time	*Lots of Time*
*Use a lunch period or common prep. Set a timer for half of the time so you still keep some of the time for a break or for individual prep, as needed. *Use time before or after school. Bring food or meet in a local restaurant to make it more of a mix of work and pleasure. *If you cannot meet in person, use Google or Zoom, or another sharing platform to communicate at times that are convenient.	*Consider plotting out a long-term plan for your meetings. Set both long- and short-term goals and check in periodically to see how well you are progressing. *Make time to meet with other collaborative teams to share progress and ask for feedback.
Faculty Culture	
Limited Interest in Collaboration	*Lots of Interest in Collaboration*
*Find one collaborator. It only takes one person to foster amazing collaboration! *Focus on common goals of students because you have to come together to do what's best for the students. *If you are part of a hiring committee, make collaboration a priority. During the hiring process, dig in to see what the candidate will do to add to the collaborative group. If you are not on a hiring committee, ask those who are on the committee for this to be a priority.	*What can you do to make your classroom, school, and community better? *How can you involve students, school personnel, families, and community members in your collaborative planning?

WHY I LIKE THIS STRATEGY

"You get to see a lot of different perspectives on things—things that people try in their classroom that work for particular students or how a colleague might respond to an email or to a challenging student. There's lots of collaboration and ideas."

—*Tina Tuminaro*

"EVERY voice is heard, and all of our opinions are valued. Collaborative planning also allows us to have a common language and goals for our scholars."

—*Emilio Burgos*

STRATEGY IN ACTION: COLLABORATIVE REFLECTION TO INFORM PLANNING

"This year I am teaching one of two sections of second grade. The other section is taught by a fellow founding member of the school. We value our common planning time to look at our units of study in all subjects and reflect on their placements and the amount of time we have allocated for each subject. We are both very 'scheduled' people, so we agree to block out 50 minutes on Wednesdays. This is when we close our door and look at our units and UbD for literacy and see how the students are navigating the essential questions and the skills required for each unit. We think through 'how are they understanding this . . . ?' 'What aspect will be mastered?' 'How will this final product look with these understandings?' 'How can we rework this path to allow for multiple entry points?' 'Is this still the allotted time frame? Do we need to extend the time frame to include some "reteaching"?' 'How is this working this year, did we notice any points, vocabulary, or helpful tools that we can incorporate for next year?' This time is dedicated throughout the year and we try to keep our units up-to-date as much as possible.

We then use what we gather from our meetings to meet with the grades before and after us to disclose our findings and what we feel could support their teaching and their students' learning."

—*Emilio Burgos*

STRATEGY 8: USING ASSESSMENTS TO GUIDE INSTRUCTION

Chapter Contributors
Katherine O'Sullivan, Bay Shore Middle School (NY), 7th grade
Diedre Downing, NYC iSchool (NY), 9th grade

Use formal and informal assessments to guide planning based on students' Knowledge/Skills/Dispositions (K/S/D). This may be done on a large or small scale with short- or long-term goals. For instance, you might use a diagnostic assessment that leads to individual learning pathways to support student mastery in topics and/or use a short, informal assessment at the end of class to determine adjustments for subsequent lessons.

STRATEGY IMPLEMENTATION

1. *Focus on Objectives*—Consider the objectives for the unit and the learning experiences you are developing. Think about:
   - The K/S/D you want your students to develop
   - How these K/S/D correlate with standards and assessment
   - How the learning experiences you are designing help students meet or exceed the unit objectives
2. *Select Your Mode of Assessment*—Decide which assessment(s) will be most useful for you. Consider:
   - What you know about students' K/S/D from prior units' formative and summative assessments
   - Diagnostic assessments that will hone in on the baseline of students' K/S/D for the unit
   - Formative assessments that will show growth over time
   - Summative assessment options that highlight students' K/S/D through varied means
3. *Assess Your Students*—Remember that assess means "to sit beside." This is not about earning a grade or a high score. How does the approach you chose enable you to "sit beside" each student to gather a sense of how they are developing their K/S/D? When you assess, contemplate:
   - The K/S/D that students are developing
   - The K/S/D that are challenging for students
   - The ways students have met or exceeded K/S/D objectives
   - Whether you need to grade the assessment, and if so, how to ensure the grading does not impede authentic student answers

> "You may be surprised by what students show you on the spot and without the pressure of a formal assessment; what students produce for an informal assessment may be different from what they do during more formal assessments."
>
> —*Katherine O'Sullivan*

Ideas for Assessing Students

When you are thinking about assessment options, think about modes of assessment that have worked well with your students in the past and new modes of assessment that will reveal students' strengths, areas for improvement, and opportunities to take the learning further.

Diagnostic Assessments

**Google Form Survey*—Use Google Forms to create a pre-test for students. This should represent varied levels of K/S/D so you can assess where students are in their learning prior to the start of the unit.

**K/W/L Chart*—Students brainstorm individually or in groups *what they know* ("K") and *want to know* ("W") regarding the K/S/D of the unit. After the unit, they complete the *what they learned* ("L") section. You may want to add an "A" section for *and*, which focuses on what students still want to learn and what they learned that was not part of the objectives.

Formative Assessments

**Sticky Notes*—Use sticky notes for students to respond to a question that helps you measure student progress. Students may place their responses to the question in one of three sections on the board—Know It, Pretty Sure, and Not Sure.

**Thumbs Up/Thumbs Down*—Use thumbs up, down, or sideways for a quick assessment of how confident students are about their understanding/abilities. Thumbs up indicates that students are confident in their knowledge/abilities, down means that they are not confident, and in the middle indicates that they are developing.

Remember: Being confident doesn't mean that students are actually understanding or doing things correctly!

4. *Plan Next Steps*—Based on what you learn about K/S/D from all of your assessments, create "learning paths"—from novice through challenging—to review/practice skills. "Learning paths" are a series of learning experiences that can be adapted based on students' needs, including video lessons, practice problems with self-assessment, mini projects, and so on. Support students during 2–3 days of individual and/or group work to prepare for a larger, full class activity or project that builds and extends skills. Focus on:
   - How to support students who are struggling
   - How to extend student learning if students have already met the K/S/D objectives
   - Where to go next if all students have met or exceeded all objectives

> "Knowing your students and what they need allows you to set up the right set of activities to meet their needs."
> —*Diedre Downing*

STRATEGY IN ACTION: ASSESSMENT AND TAILORING INSTRUCTION TO MEET INDIVIDUAL NEEDS

"I was teaching a lesson on identifying and solving equations with one unique solution, infinite solutions, or no solutions. I gave the students an equation, and they had to use algebraic reasoning to decide the number of possible solutions. This class was an accelerated seventh grade math class working on eighth grade level work. The students were happy to post their results on our giant class post-it to show what 'stuck with them' that day. After the class was over, I was able to sort their answers into categories based on their understanding (little/no understanding, partial understanding, or full understanding). Based on this, I was able to see which students needed additional support/practice, which students were right on track, and which students needed a challenge. The next day, I was able to provide the students with guidance tailored to their needs. It was particularly helpful to get feedback from my less outgoing students who were not comfortable volunteering in front of the class. It so happened that I taught this lesson on a day when I was observed, so I was also able to bring the post-it notes to my post-observation meeting to provide evidence of student understanding/assessment."

—*Katherine O'Sullivan*

HOW THIS STRATEGY MIGHT BE ADAPTED BASED ON TEACHING EXPERIENCE

Early Career Teachers

As an early career teacher, determine what your students know and don't know, then use that information to help you decide how to respond and/or seek support in planning from a mentor teacher who can help you address specific needs. It is also helpful to bring data to post-observation conferences so you can discuss your progress and your needs with your administration/instructional coaches.

Veteran Teachers

As veteran teachers, it can be too easy to fall into a routine that you think works. When using assessments to guide instruction, you are ensuring that you are not taking a one-size-fits-all approach. Work with colleagues to determine effective next steps to meet students where they are and push them to advance their K/S/D. Use your experience to guide your analysis and planning, but always keep the individual students in mind.

WHY I LIKE THIS STRATEGY

"When the students share their work, they often will show me and each other alternate ways of solving problems, which may not be obvious to the entire class. This gives the students a better understanding of the task."

—*Katherine O'Sullivan*

"I strongly believe that students learn best when they feel challenged and not overwhelmed. By acknowledging that students are at different mastery levels—due to multiple possible reasons—I take away the pressure to show mastery of a skill right away."

—*Diedre Downing*

Adaptation for Different Assets/Needs

Timing	
Limited Time *Conduct assessments in the form of an exit ticket. Have students turn their exit tickets into one of three boxes where they can self-assess their confidence in their answers: Confident, Comfortable, Confused. Then, begin the class the next day by highlighting student responses (anonymously) to show responses/approaches that were accurate/effective and responses/approaches that may need to be rethought. *Use quick assessments such as online quizzes or a question on an index card in the middle class to set up homogeneous or heterogeneous pairs/groups.	*Lots of Time* *With extra time, you can prepare more detailed or open-ended questions. *Use your time to conference with individual students regarding their progress with the K/S/D they are working to develop. Consider what successes they have had and what next steps they need to take. (See the Failing Forward Strategy in Chapter 1 for more on this.)
Technology	
Low Tech *When reviewing hard copies of student work, sort into piles based on similarities or trends in K/S/D. Use this data to guide your next steps with students. *Create stations with anchor charts that support breaking down the K/S/D and work that helps students develop. Not all students have to go to all stations. You may assign students to stations or they may self-select based on their diagnostic or formative assessment results.	*High Tech* *Use Google or a similar platform to create quizzes for diagnostic assessments and related K/S/D work based on results. *Use the Post-It App to organize students' sticky notes answers according to similarities or trends in K/S/D. *Once students have completed their work, text answers via the Remind App.

STRATEGY IN ACTION: ASSESSMENT AND SELF-DIRECTED LEARNING

"As the shift to the Common Core curriculum was getting underway in New York State, I found that the students in my geometry class were coming in with very different Algebra skills based on what their previous school had adopted for curricula/used for a cumulative examination. I personally hate teaching 'review' of concepts that students 'should have learned' previously and wanted to create an experience where students could have choice and self-direct their learning to be prepared for a larger class assignment. The first time I utilized this strategy was for preparation for an exploration into trigonometry. I wanted to honor the experiences and expertise of the students in the classroom without making other students feel like they were behind because they had not experienced introductory trigonometry topics in their previous classes. For the three days that the students worked through their own learning paths I was able to provide targeted support to each student. At the end of the self-paced (or small group) work time, I asked the students to complete a survey about the learning experience. Most students appreciated the ability to work on their own and have choice in how they engaged in the material. I decided that I would regularly work to add this type of self-directed learning into my practice after this initial trial."

—*Diedre Downing*

STRATEGY 9: INQUIRY-BASED LEARNING

Chapter Contributors
Christine Mercer, Yardville Elementary School (NJ), Pre-K–5th grade
Tobey Reed, Attleboro High School (MA), 9th–12th grade

Inquiry-based learning starts with sparking students' curiosity to learn about a topic that matters to them. Students engage in research and experimentation to address a question or problem, and they share their findings with peers and teachers. This strategy transfers responsibility from teacher to student. With the understanding that they are supported, students can take risks in their learning, discover patterns and make connections to help them grasp difficult concepts, and explore multiple solutions without the fear of finding *only one* right answer.

STRATEGY IMPLEMENTATION

Part I: Planning and Preparation

1. *Determine the Activity/Project's Big Ideas*—Develop the inquiry activity/project's essential questions, student learning objectives, evidence of student learning, and connections to state learning standards. Ensure:
   - The essence of your inquiry-based activity/project is something all your students will want to do and will find meaning in doing.
   - Your essential questions have multiple potential answers, require deep investigation, and necessitate layers of critical thinking and analysis to answer.
   - The evidence of student learning is authentic and supportive of your diverse learners.
2. *Create an Open-Ended "Problem"*—Based on your essential questions, create an open-ended problem to present to your students. Consider the questions:
   - Is the problem something all students can understand?
   - Is the problem something all students will want to get to the bottom of?
3. *Identify Resources and Materials Needed*—Decide what resources and materials are necessary to make your activity/project happen. Keep in mind what resources and/or materials:
   - You have access to in your school
   - Your students have access to at home
   - Are necessary to make the project happen
   - Would be a luxury to have
   - Are sharable
   - Can be reused and/or repurposed
4. *Determine the Method of Assessment*—Plan how you will assess or evaluate the work of students. This can be as simple as student reflection, an in-depth rubric, or written or verbal feedback. Ask yourself:
   - What is the best way to assess students for this activity/project?
   - What type of feedback is best to support students for this activity/project?

5. *Write Up Your Activity/Project*—Once you have determined your big ideas, created one open-ended problem, and determined the necessary materials, write up your project and break down the steps of the students' investigation. Make sure to:
   - Scaffold the steps of investigation in a way that is developmentally appropriate for your students.
   - Differentiate the project in necessary ways to support the different learners in your classroom.

Part II: Introducing and Executing the Plan

1. *Introduce the Activity/Project*—Take the necessary time to introduce the activity/project so all students are clear about expectations and what to do before they begin. Do the following:
   - Provide *Instructions Three Ways*: (1) orally with the whole class, (2) projected or written on the board, and (3) on paper/computer in front of the students.
   - Review the assignment, have students reinforce what they have to do, and answer any student questions.
   - If you have time, give students (once in groups) a chance to discuss the activity/project and develop any additional questions they have to pose in front of the class.
   - Once all questions have been answered, have students begin.

> Determining Groups
> - Keep groups between three and five students.
> - Decide whether groups will be random, strategically created, or student selected. (Consider academics, personality, interests, skills, and talents when configuring groups.)
> - Determine roles for each group member for which the amount of work is equitable and the roles require all students to be working at all times. (See Base Group roles on page 14 for ideas about possible roles.)

2. *Give Students Time to Explore*—It is important to allow groups space and time to explore the problem on their own with built-in scaffolds and support from the teacher. This can be done in one day or across multiple days. Some strategies include:
   - Prepare prompting/guiding questions for your students.
   - Use work time to conference with groups and individual students.
   - Scaffold/chunk the exploration so students have clear guidelines and targets to support their exploration.

3. *Share and Debrief*—Give students time to explain their findings. They can elaborate on what they have found by leading a discussion with a small group or the class. This is a great time to engage in critical reflection about where students and their groups are in the process of their exploration.

4. *Revise and Move Toward a Solution*—Have students take the feedback they received from their peers and revise their work as they move toward their solution to the problem.
   - Provide guiding questions and graphic organizers to support the revision process.
   - Ensure students are relying on analysis of evidence to come up with and support their solution.

5. *Final Product*—Provide students with clear expectations for the final product they are producing (rubric or other template). Make sure:
   - The final product reflects the work of the *entire group* and *individual contributions.*
   - Groups share their findings.
   - The whole class engages in debates/discussions around different solutions to the "problem."

Part III: Assessing and Reflecting

1. *Assess Individuals and Groups*—For any group work, determine how you can assess the group as a whole as well as each member of the group. Consider:
   - What components of the activity/project reflect *individual student work* that you can effectively assess
   - What criteria you can use to assess the entire *group*
   - Whether students should self-assess their *individual* and *group* performance and their mastery of the content/skills

2. *Critical Reflection*—Reflect on the lesson or the project. What went well? What did not go well? Think about what you might want to change if you were to teach this again. Make sure both the students and you as the teacher can critically reflect on the process and product of the activity/project.

STRATEGY IN ACTION: LISTEN TO YOUR STUDENTS TO MAKE YOUR INQUIRY PROJECT BETTER

"This year is my first year teaching seniors in Level III Criminal Justice. I have had them for two years prior, so they are very attuned to how we work as a class. One of the things that we were working on was a senior project. I had written up a project packet with all sorts of steps that they would work on and a rationale on why they were doing it. We started working on it, spending a day or so every week working on one aspect or another. After a few months, I noticed that the excitement just wasn't there. They were not into the project. So, we circled the desks and had a mid-course check in.

It was fascinating. They did not think that this project culminated all of their learning. So they explained what they wanted to do instead, which was to select their own criminal justice issues and then analyze them through videotaped scenarios that explored their decision-making processes. Students videotaped themselves acting out a scenario such as a motor vehicle stop or medical emergency. Each 10–15 minute scenario involved 'game-time decisions.' Students wrote up reports regarding their decision-making, and they presented their projects to a panel of outside judges who worked in criminal justice.

This new project achieved the same goals as the original project, and it was more rigorous than what I designed. Students knew they had some agency on what they were learning and how they were learning it."

—*Tobey Reed*

HOW THIS STRATEGY MIGHT BE ADAPTED BASED ON TEACHING EXPERIENCE

Early Career Teachers

Start small. Focus on a topic that you and your students are passionate about. This will help to ensure buy-in. Ask for help. Is there a colleague that you can partner with to make this inquiry activity/project interdisciplinary or something that involves more than one class?

Veteran Teachers

Take risks! Try new styles of inquiry activities/projects that challenge you as a teacher and will extend your students' learning. Think of ways to adapt and improve inquiry-based activities and projects you have used for many years.

WHY I LIKE THIS STRATEGY

"Students should be active learners and take responsibility for their own learning. Inquiry-based learning allows students to create, find patterns, and make connections with what they are learning about. When planning for inquiry-based lessons, you know students will have a deep understanding of the topic, while being highly engaged. In the beginning of the year, it is imperative you get to know your students' strengths and weaknesses. It is important to plan for differentiation among the tasks (low floor, high ceiling), which can often be time-consuming and difficult. However, the work you put into planning pays off. The responsibility of learning shifts to the students. Teachers play more of a guide, questioning students and conferencing. Your day feels easier as you are doing significantly less talking and lecturing."

—*Christine Mercer*

CONSIDERING DIFFERENT TYPES OF LEARNERS

Inquiry-Based Learning can be adapted for different types of learners:

1. *English Language Learners* can work with materials in their preferred language if the objective is skills/content-based. Alternatively, they may work with reading materials that are appropriate to their language abilities.
2. Inquiry-based activities and projects can be scaffolded to varying degrees to support authentic discovery by *Special Education* students. Keep the learning challenging but accessible for the students!
3. *Gifted and Talented* students may apply their strengths to determine next steps with inquiry-based learning. Whatever adaptations you make for gifted and talented students, be sure they are about deepening the meaning of their work rather than adding on more busy work.

Adaptation for Different Assets/Needs

Class Size	
Small Class	*Large Class*
*Have more teacher conferences with students and groups. *Have each group share and critique their findings with the class (since it will take less time with fewer groups). *Provide opportunities for students to reflect on the connections among their inquiry experiences and the Knowledge/Skills/Dispositions they are developing.	*Ensure you are able to share resources between groups, so each group has access to the necessary resources. *Aim for more long-term inquiry projects so there is a greater opportunity for groups to share resources. *Have several small groups (3–5 students) rather than a few large groups. *Have groups compare and contrast with other groups (since it will take lots of time to have every group present in front of the class to do critical debriefs).
Technology	
Low Tech	*High Tech*
*Use print resources like books and articles to expose students to topics. *Encourage students to survey stakeholders related to the topic or interview experts. *Focus on cultivating students' creativity of solutions.	*Teach how to utilize multiple platforms (web, print, social media, etc.). *Use shared folders and documents (like Google Drive).

STRATEGY IN ACTION: STUDENT-INITIATED INQUIRY

"Our class was reading an article about the bombing of Pearl Harbor in a unit focused on synthesizing. As we were reading, the class started bombarding me with questions about World War II. I began answering them, but after the first few questions, it felt like I was doing a lot of work. I thought to myself, 'Why aren't my students answering these questions?' That's when I stopped answering their questions and had them record them on sticky notes to place on the wall.

After we finished reading the article, I had students choose a question they were interested in. We went to the library to find books, watched interviews with historians, and explored online resources to find the answers to our questions. The students were so actively engaged in reading articles, taking notes, and creating a presentation about what they learned. Even though we weren't doing my planned lessons on synthesizing, they were doing just that! They took information from all their sources to create and learn something new. Students presented their work and answered questions their classmates had. They essentially became the teachers. The motivation to learn and the engagement was clear each day as students busily worked and after seeing their effort and smiles while presenting their end results."

—*Christine Mercer*

STRATEGY 10: CULTURALLY RESPONSIVE/ SUSTAINING TEACHING

Chapter Contributors
Naeem Muse, Luis Munoz Rivera Community Middle School (NJ), 8th grade
Ashley Warren, West Windsor HS North (NJ), 9th–12th grade

Culturally Responsive/Sustaining Teaching (CRT) takes into account the academic, social, and cultural knowledge that students bring to the classroom. Students' cultures and backgrounds are seen as assets—not deficits—in the classroom. Teachers design the learning environment with students at the center, and teachers work to promote equity in the classroom and justice in the world.

The Power of Getting to Know Your Students!

"Culturally Responsive/Sustaining Teaching is grounded in building relationships while increasing students' self-worth in the classroom. Many low-income students have negative experiences in school due to a lack of cultural appropriateness, professional development for staff, environmental challenges, etc. Most curricula are set up to empower the American majority. Students develop a lack of trust and motivation when the person speaking, the teacher, can't relate to or at least understand what he or she, the student, may be experiencing. There is a saying that a teacher should 'know their audience.' A teacher shouldn't only 'know their audience,' he or she should become 'part of the audience' as well."

—*Naeem Muse*

STRATEGY IMPLEMENTATION

Part I: Understanding *Who* is in Your Classroom—Before planning CRT, it is important to understand who is in your classroom and how to best prepare to support *each* of your students.

1. *Recognize Multiple Cultures Exist in Your Class (at Any Given Time)*—Within every classroom, the following cultures exist:
   - *Classroom Culture*—The culture in your classroom that you, as a teacher, must create to make the students feel safe and wanted
   - *Student Culture*—The culture each student brings from home; their

Questions to Ask Yourself about Recognizing Cultures in Your Classroom

- What do you already know about each of these cultures?
- What preconceived notions/beliefs might you hold regarding any of these cultures?
- How can you gain more information about each culture?
- How can you shift your mindset to ensure you are focusing on the assets of your students and their communities?

instilled family values and belief systems
- *Community Culture*—The norms and practices within the students' community where you teach

"Whenever you speak about someone's culture, you have to speak greatness into it."

—*Naeem Muse*

2. *Research Students' Cultures*—Finds ways to research the cultural backgrounds of each of your students to get to know them better and ensure you don't perpetuate stereotypes. This shows the student you have a personal interest in him or her. Consider:
   - The most effective way to identify the cultural backgrounds of your students
   - The best way to learn from your students about their cultural backgrounds (e.g., talking to them, asking them questions, assigning projects related to their culture)
   - What you can read about your students' cultural backgrounds and how you can ensure a diversity of sources in learning about their backgrounds

"As they 'teach the teacher,' the students will feel empowered. 'Wow, I know something the teacher doesn't know!'"

—*Naeem Muse*

Tips for Building a Strong Classroom Climate!

- Start at the beginning of the year (so they don't think you're being phony).
- Create norms as a class that guide your interactions (See Strategy 1: Group Agreements and Strategy 2: Establishing Routines).
- Ensure there is mutual respect among all people in your classroom. This may take time, "calling out" when respect is not occurring, and talking collectively about how "we" can work toward mutual respect (don't make it about an individual or individuals).
- Acknowledge and value the perspectives of others.
- Allow students to address you using positive names.

"Instead of Mr. Muse, sometimes it morphs into Dad, Uncle Muse, Pop, etc. This is an expression of love and respect from the students in my community. The students will use terms of endearment, so allow them. This usually happens according to their cultural background."

—*Naeem Muse*

- *Let students know you LOVE them EVERYDAY* upon leaving the class. This is your expression of gratitude, and kids know someone loves them.
- Don't be afraid to open up to your students and give personal real-life situations you may have experienced that could relate to their current circumstances (e.g., death in the family, someone going to jail, moving to a new area, educational background, family background, etc.).

"Most students are excited to learn that I grew up in a rough part of Trenton and I still live around them in the city. Share yourself with the students."

—*Naeem Muse*

3. *Build Relationships with/between Your Students*—Find ways to integrate relationship building (teacher-student and student-student relationships) *during your class time*. Consider:
   - Relationship building activities you can integrate into lessons.
   - Spaces during lessons that lend themselves to relationship building.
   - Ways to sustain relationship building in your classroom throughout the year.

   Additionally, you can *use nontraditional times* for relationship building, such as:

   - Inviting students to eat lunch in your classroom to talk with them about non-school-related things or stopping them in the hallway to do the same.
   - Attending extracurricular activities (it shows you are interested in their life).
   - Listening to students' music, likes, and dislikes.

Part II: Planning for Your Classroom—Once you have learned about the cultural backgrounds of your students, you must be strategic about how you integrate that knowledge into your practice.

1. *Create Engaging Assignments That Empower Students of All Backgrounds*—Use your knowledge of your students' backgrounds to create assignments that celebrate your students' cultures and connect with your students' lived experiences. Make sure to:
   - Connect students' cultural backgrounds with class content.
   - Focus on individuals that demonstrate and celebrate aspects of students' cultures.
   - Find readings/texts that are responsive to the backgrounds of your students.
   - Be inclusive of all your students by discussing multiple viewpoints when certain class texts and topics align more with particular student backgrounds.

> "Students need to see themselves as positive and/or powerful figures in history for them to be interested. Find information and historical figures in each subject which the students can relate to in their personal life whether that person looks like them or dealt with a similar situation. The information is out there, but the educator must dig deep!"
>
> —*Naeem Muse*

2. *Personalize Student Learning*—Consider student interests, backgrounds, and lived experiences when you develop learning objectives and learning experiences and design assessments to represent student growth.

3. *Ensure Class Texts Are Diverse*—Read and study works created by diverse authors and artists. These can be texts that align with your students'

> Making CRT Work in Math/Science!
> - Embed CRT into instructional choices more than the content.
> - Stress classroom norms and create an atmosphere that celebrates differences, multiple perspectives, and teamwork.
> - Create projects and assessments that are grounded in real-world connections that align with your students' experiences and backgrounds.

cultural backgrounds as well as texts that expose students to unfamiliar cultural backgrounds.

4. *Show and Tell*—Regularly bring in artifacts that students can touch and learn about. Encourage students to bring in artifacts to discuss. As Naeem Muse noted, "We are never too old for show and tell."

Part III: Implementing Your CRT Plan—Once you have done the work of creating a strong classroom culture, built strong relationships with and among students, and strategically planned ways to integrate students' cultural backgrounds into your class, be intentional in how you implement your CRT plan.

1. *Greet Your Students*—Stand outside the classroom and greet each student as they enter the room. Do this on a daily basis to set the tone for your time together. When greeting students, ensure you:
   - View facial expressions and body language to get a quick gauge of each student's mental and physical well-being.
   - Be relaxed and let the students know that you are happy to see them. Especially the student that may be more challenging than most.
2. *Sharing Cultural Backgrounds/Identities*—When integrating assignments and experiences that help students explore their own and others' cultural backgrounds, build in time and exercises that support students sharing their backgrounds and identities with one another. Consider:
   - What activities allow students to share their cultural backgrounds and identities in a respectful way.
   - How you will prepare the class to share personal information about themselves and learn about others' backgrounds.

> "You would be surprised how much you learn about a student and their family by just allowing students to talk. . . . Be part of the audience."
>
> —*Naeem Muse*

3. *Ensure Every Student Is Heard*—Every child wants to be heard, so listen to what they have to say even if it seems unimportant or uninteresting to you. Be sure to:
   - Prioritize class time for students to share their stories.
   - Let students tell their story without interruption.
   - Give constant feedback and respond to their life stories.
4. *Use "We Messages"*—Using "we messages" makes everyone feel included and part of a collective community. In particular, with this inclusive way of speaking and addressing the class, withdrawn and quiet students and students whose behavior may be in question are reminded in a gentle manner what is and is not acceptable. "We messages" also make students accountable for each other's actions and eventually students will address each other's actions without teacher involvement. "We messages" include:
   - When explaining something to the class, say "Today *we* are going to . . ."
   - If someone does something wrong, say "*We* don't do that in here."

5. *Take Action against Injustice*—Name injustices you see and hear in the classroom and discuss ways to overcome them (or ways that people have already worked to overcome them). This might include topics covered within your content OR when students say or do things that are hurtful, perpetuate stereotypes, and/or go against the class norms and expectations. When addressing injustices in your classroom, make sure to:
   - Figure out how to directly and respectfully address the injustice.
   - Determine a tangible action against the injustice that will have a direct impact on the lives of your students.
   - Consider which class projects are most effective in connecting classroom content with actions students can take that relate to effect change in their lives.

Creating an Environment Open to Difference

- Introduce controversy that is low stakes (chocolate vs. vanilla; basketball vs. baseball, etc.) and have students engage in a friendly debate.
- Set ground rules for a respectful debate, including: wait until the person is done speaking; respond directly to what the person said rather than the person's character; use "I heard you say" statements; offer alternatives or solutions grounded in evidence.
- Gradually introduce higher-stakes controversy into the classroom.
- Once students are ready, have students explore personal topics they initially only share with the teacher.
- Share in a low-stakes way (e.g., gallery walk with sticky note feedback). Then reflect on the experience of sharing and commenting on that information and debrief as a class about the process.
- Gradually scale up to activities and sharing that challenge students to open up more about their backgrounds and learn more about their peers.

WHY I LIKE THIS STRATEGY

"Education in the US is both a right and a public good. My role as a teacher is to see that all of my students have access to that right and that all of my students can benefit from that public good, especially students who have been denied that right and good in the past. In my classroom, I work to ensure that all of my students are welcomed, seen, valued, served, challenged, and supported. Ultimately, I hope to promote a vision of social justice in my classroom that overflows into the world."

—*Ashley Warren*

HOW THIS STRATEGY MIGHT BE ADAPTED BASED ON TEACHING EXPERIENCE

Early Career Teachers

Get to know your students well and then gradually integrate that knowledge into your curriculum. Remember, CRT starts with building strong relationships with your students. Also, visit teachers who thrive at creating culturally responsive/sustaining classrooms.

Veteran Teachers

If CRT is something new to you, examine your curriculum to see where you can best integrate information that reflects the backgrounds of your students. Then, take the time you need to get to know them and do the integration! Also, don't be shy about visiting other teachers who thrive with CRT, even if they are newer to teaching than you.

STRATEGY IN ACTION: DISPELLING STEREOTYPES IN A HIGH SCHOOL SPANISH CLASS

"In my Stereotypes, Discrimination, & Tolerance Unit, my Spanish 3 students discussed common stereotypes from the past and present. We studied how various people have experienced discrimination, and we researched ways that people have overcome discrimination and promoted tolerance and justice in the world. Some activities included: listening to native Spanish speakers discuss the stereotypes that they most wish were eliminated from the world, choosing different 'Human Rights Heroes' and studying how these leaders worked to promote peace, reading excerpts from an immigrant's autobiography (*When I used to be Puerto Rican*), and watching the movie *Almost a Woman* about a Puerto Rican teen's education in New York. Towards the end of the unit, students created a sign that dispelled a stereotype that others believe about them and posed for a picture with the sign. Students then presented their photo to the class and shared how they felt identifying and dispelling a stereotype about themselves. Finally, students wrote about the experience and connected their reflections to what they learned from the authentic products (movies, audios, readings, etc.) reviewed in class."

—*Ashley Warren*

CONSIDERING DIFFERENT TYPES OF LEARNERS

CRT can be adapted for different types of learners:

1. *English Language Learners (ELLs)* might have a more difficult time understanding connections you are trying to make because of a language barrier. But, through strong relationship building and finding alternative means of communication (visuals, translations, etc.), ELLs will feel empowered to see themselves in the curriculum and honored within the class.

2. For *all students*, but in particular ELLs, Special Education students, and students with low self-esteem (and other nonclassified students), it is important to focus on student strengths and not deficits.
3. Students of *all ages* can be positively impacted by CRT; however, for *younger students*, their conceptual understanding of CRT is very different from older students. Younger students might not be aware of differences or have the vocabulary to describe or name them. Therefore, begin by focusing on physical differences and acknowledging the beauty in those differences. Gradually work toward more conceptual understandings of difference.

What My Students Get Out of a Culturally Responsive/Sustaining Classroom

- Students see themselves in history and it becomes interesting
- Increases motivation to learn
- Empowers each student about their ancestry
- Teaches leadership skills
- Increases understanding and respect for peers of diverse background
- Increases classroom engagement
- Students are more apt to share detrimental personal information.

—*Naeem Muse*

STRATEGY IN ACTION: THE IMPACT OF USING CRT IN AN URBAN MIDDLE SCHOOL

"One morning I was standing outside the classroom greeting the students as they entered the class. I could see that one student was visibly upset as if she wanted to cry but was holding it in. As she passed, I calmly said, 'hey stay right here with me for a minute, I have to talk to you about something.' I told her that I could see that something was wrong and asked what I could do to help. She explained that she overheard some students talking about how she better not leave her bookbag in the room because everyone might die. The student wore a Hijab to school, everyday, and was visibly an African Muslim.

That day I planned to teach about Feudalism but the concerns of students are more important than 'planned lessons.' I knew I had to use this situation to create a teaching moment. I told her not to worry because after today her peers would understand how great she was. She smiled and said thank you. As I entered the class, I didn't address them about what the young lady told me. I simply said, 'Grab your chromebooks. I want you all to research 5 Islamic inventions.' As the kids researched, I could hear them say, 'Oh my God! They discovered coffee!?' I replied, 'yes, if it wasn't for them Mr. Muse would be a horrible teacher. . . . I need my coffee.' More kids exclaimed, 'They invented the first flying machine!,' 'They invented chess! I love chess!,' 'They invented ritual bathing and cleanliness!,' The first clock, camera, university, quilting, etc.!

Students began to say that, 'Wow Muslims were really smart. How did they do all that so long ago?!' As this was taking place, I could see the young Muslim girl in the class lifting her head in pride. One of the students even said to the young girl, 'that's probably why you're so smart!' Of course, she replied 'yes.' I then asked the students to write a story about what life would be like without these wonderful Islamic inventions. The kids were excited about the assignment. The students began to ask the young Muslim girl about her experiences in life, her religion and traditions. She felt empowered as she answered their questions. I told the class that if they would like to come back up for lunch to learn more, they could.

Most students came back up and we discussed Islam and how beautiful it is. We discussed terrorism and how it comes in ALL forms from ALL cultures. We discussed how Muslims have been demonized. We discussed what their parents teach them at home versus what they learn from me. The student asked me if she could teach the class more about her culture. I'm a firm believer that a person must 'strike while the kettle is hot!' The next class she brought in artifacts and taught the class how she prays five times a day as well as many other Islamic traditions and holidays. From that day forward many students came to lunch to discuss social issues and personal problems. We developed a trust and a bond as a community and began to celebrate each other's differences."

—*Naeem Muse*

Adaptation for Different Assets/Needs

Teaching Persona/Personality	
Reserved/Strict	*Outgoing/Humorous*
*Learn about the class population and find spaces for students to read about themselves and come up with activities that completely engage the students. *Make activities very student-centered that use the student energy. The right student-centered activity will change the energy of the room. *Instead of being a teacher on stage, come up with ways to help students speak with each other in class.	*Use your "stage" to acknowledge and celebrate the different cultural backgrounds in your classroom. *Create student-centered activities that challenge students to speak with one another.
Sharing Cultural Background with Students	
Similar Cultural Background	*Different Cultural Background*
*Share your stories with your students and make connections with their lived experiences. *Focus on getting to know, understand, and appreciate differences that still exist between and among people in your classroom. *Identify and spend time learning about and celebrating cultures and identities that are different from those within the classroom.	*Share your stories with your students and help them get to know you while you ask to learn about their lived experiences. *Celebrate similarities and differences between your background and your students. *Be committed to becoming "part of the audience" and "the community." Get to know the neighborhood, the people within it, and attend community events (among other things).

Chapter 3

Instructional Strategies

This chapter explores the following instructional strategies:

- *Deepening Discussions* to engage all students on multiple levels (Strategy 11)
- Utilizing *Small Group Stations* to have students work through diverse materials and develop specific K/S/D at each station (Strategy 12)
- *Arts Integration* to diversify and energize student learning and routines (Strategy 13)
- Using *Mock Trials* to engage students in the analysis of multiple perspectives around controversial issues (Strategy 14)
- Incorporating *Student Self-Assessment* into your instruction so students can take more control of their own learning and growth (Strategy 15)

Building on Strategies 9 and 10, which focus on the transition from planning to implementation, this chapter focuses explicitly on instructional strategies you can integrate into your daily lessons. Each of the strategies highlights different components of instruction that can complement various pedagogical styles.

HELPFUL UNDERSTANDINGS

This chapter utilizes larger frames and ideas that you will see referenced often.

Teacher as Facilitator (Student-Centered Instruction)

Many people enter teaching because of their passion for a particular content area as well as a love of working with children. However, that passion for content can lead to teachers dominating the discussion in their classrooms and making the classroom more teacher-centered than student-centered. The strategies in this chapter focus on helping support the teacher as a *facilitator* of student learning.

Think about all of the dynamics in your classroom that impact student engagement and learning. As Lampert (2001) stated, "In classrooms, students have relationships with one another over content. When they act in the public space of the classroom, they also teach one another, deliberately or not. By structuring relationships among students to support appropriate learning, a teacher in a classroom can add to [their] practical resources" (p. 425). By expanding your idea of what and how students are learning in the classroom, it will be easier to see yourself more as a facilitator of student K/S/D.

Additionally, it is important to contemplate your power within the classroom and how that impacts the teacher-student dynamic and student engagement. To do that, you can join democratic teachers who "tend to create classrooms where students are empowered and effective in working on academic and social problems. Openness, high levels of communication, independent thinking, and internal motivation are the hallmarks of the democratic classroom" (Schmuck & Schmuck, 2001, 235).

In the strategy overviews that follow in this chapter, you will read about ways to make learning more student-centered through discussion, stations, small groups, projects, and self-assessments.

Teacher as Facilitator Highlights

- Get advice on how to integrate multiple voices into your classroom discussions in *Deepening Discussions* (Strategy 11).
- In *Small Group Stations* (Strategy 12), see seven explicit tips on how teachers can facilitate student success with stations.
- Learn about ways that students choose songs to support transitions between activities in *Arts Integration* (Strategy 13).
- In *Mock Trials* (Strategy 14), see how to scaffold students' roles to support students' exploration of multiple perspectives on controversial topics.

Integrating Culturally Responsive/Sustaining Teaching into Instruction

As noted in the book's introduction, this entire book is grounded in culturally responsive/sustaining practices. Regardless of your content area, the age of students you teach, or where you teach, knowing, understanding, and embracing who your students are is critical to creating and sustaining engaging and successful classrooms. Throughout this chapter, you will see strategies for implementing culturally responsive/sustaining practices in your classroom.

Culturally Responsive/Sustaining Teaching Highlights

- In *Deepening Discussion* (Strategy 11), learn how using "one mic" can help students feel empowered.
- Pay attention to how *Mock Trials* (Strategy 14) can expose students to career options and job skills through their roles in the trial.
- Note how the use of a "self-assessment scorecard" or "large-scale weekly wall survey" in *Student Self-Assessment* (Strategy 15) can be used to help your students consider their understanding, skills, and participation for the day and week.

Chunking the Lesson for Maximum Engagement

As you explore each strategy in this chapter, remember how important it is to break up your lesson into several engaging experiences rather than one long experience. Students' attention spans are short (as are adults'!); and therefore, teachers must break up lessons into manageable parts that are engaging and that flow and connect well with one another. Think about mixing up the type of activity; consider how long each activity is, and ensure that each activity builds onto the next.

GUIDING QUESTIONS

As you read through this chapter, consider the following:

- How can I work toward becoming more of a facilitator in my classroom?
- How am I incorporating culturally responsive/sustaining teaching in my instruction?
- What are the best ways for me to chunk my lessons and activities?
- How can I further deepen discussions in my classroom?
- Where can I best integrate small group stations into my instruction?
- What types of art integration can I consistently integrate into my practice?
- Are there particular topics or issues I teach that are well suited to be turned into a mock trial? What roles could expose students to career options and hone their K/S/D?
- What types of student self-assessments will work best for my students? When and where can I integrate student self-assessments into my units and lessons?

STRATEGY 11: DEEPENING DISCUSSIONS

Chapter Contributors
Jeanne Muzi, Slackwood Elementary School (NJ), Principal
Sarah Gibson, MS 88 (NY), 7th grade

Establishing routines for classroom discussions ensures that all student thinking is considered. There are several approaches that can be varied in the classroom. The common elements of these approaches include posing clear questions, giving time for students to think, listening respectfully, and staying open to multiple responses that build on and/or challenge one another.

STRATEGY IMPLEMENTATION

1. *Develop Clear and Engaging Questions*—Whether you are planning questions ahead of time or posing them organically during conversation, consider the following:
   - Are you using language that is appropriate and understandable for your students?
   - Can you answer your own question?
   - How does this question help further develop students' Knowledge/Skills/Dispositions (KSD)?
   - How have you considered students' thinking and questions?
   - Have you clarified information based on students' questions?
   - How are students' questions pushing the class forward?
2. *Wait Time*—Optimal wait time is 5–10 seconds. On average, most teachers wait 0.7 seconds for a response to a question (Teacher Vision, 2015)! Here are some tips for sticking to wait time and getting used to a few more seconds of awkward silence:
   - Explain to students that thinking is more important than speed and that their responses will be more valuable if they take the time to think. To support that, wait at least 5 seconds before calling on a student to respond to a question, and wait until multiple students are raising their hands.
   - Practice sitting in silence. Address the awkwardness and the benefits.
   - Keep yourself busy by demonstrating a silent count down. Use your hand starting with five fingers and slowly counting down to a fist. This can be the indicator that it is now OK to raise hands.

> Lead Time
>
> Lead time can help with wait time. Give students questions ahead of time so they can grapple with big ideas and come prepared to discuss. This will give the class more unique answers because students will think for themselves before they take one another's answers.
>
> You can practice on-the-spot lead time by engaging students in "Quick Writes" during which students take 30–60 seconds to jot down their answers or a "Think-Pair-Share" when students take time to think independently, share with a peer, and then share with the full class.

Moving from Cold Calling to Warm Calling

If you see a student who seems to have something to share, it is OK to *cold call*. Remember, cold calling isn't as chilly if you have developed clear and engaging questions and given adequate lead time or wait time. Then it is *warm calling*! With *warm calling*, you can encourage a student to share by pointing out that you noticed something great about their work when you were circulating the classroom or monitoring work on Google Classroom, thus making them feel more empowered to talk.

3. *Gathering Multiple Voices*—Too often in classrooms, conversations are among the teacher and a select few students who are eager to respond. Wait time can wait time can help more students to engage and respond. Below are several other ways to ensure that students feel comfortable sharing and listening respectfully to their peers:
   - *Establish a "One Mic" Approach*—Students agree that only one voice can be heard at a time, so they envision an imaginary microphone in the hands of the speaker. This is the only person who should be talking.
   - *Use a Mic Prop*—Make the "one mic" approach more tangible by using a physical prop like a ball or small pillow. The person holding the prop is the speaker.
   - *Use Popsicle Sticks or Poker Chips*—As students speak, they hand in a stick/chip. Agree on the protocol. Once your chips are in, you cannot talk again until all other students have thrown in their chips. Alternatively, you can do rounds by color (e.g., student cannot speak a second time until all of the red chips are in the bucket. Then students cannot speak a third time until all of the blue chips are in, etc.)
   - *Map the Conversation*—Give a seating chart and ask one student to draw lines from speaker to speaker. Warning! You may realize that you are doing too much talking as the teacher! Try to have at least one student follow up with a question or comment before you add to the conversation.

4. *Building/Challenging*—Getting more students involved in conversation is important; so is ensuring that students are truly listening and benefiting from the conversation. To help students make their listening and thinking clear, encourage them to make overt connections to what others have said.

   > Before students get comfortable building on one another's ideas, try to facilitate dialogue by asking the student "WHY" they said what they did and then ask other students to respond directly to the student's answer to "WHY."

   - To help students build on one another's ideas try these prompts:
     - I understand __________. Will you tell me more about *WHY*?
     - I'm thinking about what _______said about . . .
     - I want to connect with _____________'s idea that . . .
     - Building on what __________said, I think . . .

- To help students challenge one another respectfully try these:
    - Can you clarify what you meant by_____________?
    - I understand how you might think___________. Have you considered ___________?
    - I want to better understand. What evidence can you show me to support _________?
- Work with students to develop sentence starters that will make connections overt and challenging other ideas respectful. Post these where all can see.

Encouraging Risks

Some students struggle with sharing when they aren't 100 percent sure an answer is correct or when there is more than one clear answer. Having respectful ways of supporting discussion and building on thinking can help students feel more confident taking risks and answering questions even if they are unsure. Students will know they have an opportunity to explain and expand on their thinking.

5. *Reflecting on Conversations*—Provide time for students to reflect on their participation in class conversations. Encourage students to ask themselves:

    - What skills did you demonstrate well?
    - What skills need more development?
    - What new ideas did you learn?
    - How did you present a new perspective?

    See Figure 3.1.

CONSIDERING DIFFERENT TYPES OF LEARNERS

Discussion routines can be adapted for different types of learners:

1. *English Language Learners* might benefit from knowing when you will call on them. Give them a hint to prepare to share their answers about a specific topic so they can practice and build confidence.
2. *Special Education* students will benefit especially from consistent wait time. Consider giving a student the role of holding you accountable. If you start rushing through wait time, let that student be in charge of reminding you to get back to it!
3. *Gifted and Talented* students may struggle with changing the pace of the class and giving time for more students to share. Remind them that thinking is valued over speed. Challenge them to share ways that their thinking is enhanced by hearing new perspectives.

STRATEGY IN ACTION: POSE, PAUSE, POUNCE, AND BOUNCE

"I use the Pose, Pause, Pounce, and Bounce (3PB) approach with my students. I pose a question, pause to give time for thinking about the answer, pounce on a student to give a response, and bounce to other students to build on that response or pose new questions. This approach eliminates the stress for kids who may require a little bit more time to form their ideas or who are very shy and would shut down once all those 'quick hand raisers' start oohing and aahhing for the teacher's attention. 3PB brings everyone's voice in the community together in a very positive way! I would like to see more teachers using 3PB on a more regular basis, because with practice, the kids and the teacher improve in their questioning, thinking, answering and stretching their ideas. This strategy should not be pulled out for 'special' lessons or events, but should be an integral part of a teacher's questioning toolbox."

—*Jeanne Muzi*

How to Implement the Strategy at Varied GradeLevels

Elementary	*Middle*	*High*
*Use response starters and question starters to ensure supportive and meaningful conversation. *Be explicit in modeling conversation "moves" for students. Reflect on choices you make to help foster conversation so they can do the same.	*Build trust in one another so students feel OK to open up and share. *Start small (conversations in groups and easier questions that anyone could answer). Then progress to more challenging questions as the year goes on.	*Share data on the benefits of wait time. (See *The Value of Awkward Silence: Increasing Wait Time in the Classroom* excerpt in the introduction to this chapter.)

WHY I LIKE THIS STRATEGY

"If I ask one single question and one single student answers with one single 'right' answer, the other students may become discouraged, disengaged, and negative. Keeping everyone involved in developing answers and rationales for their thinking communicates the message that all of our thinking is valued and that every member of our class has a voice we want to hear."

—*Jeanne Muzi*

"I find within the cultures I teach there is a sizable population of students who prefer to remain silent. I work to balance my respect for their cultures with my desire for my students to know their voices and ideas matter; to do that, they need to value being heard."

—*Sarah Gibson*

Adaptation for Different Assets/Needs

Student Dispositions	
Quiet Students	*Talkative Students*
*Group quiet students together for classroom conversations. They may be more likely to talk among themselves. Then, as they get used to contributing, create heterogeneous groups. *Switch up small groups often early in the year so everyone gets to know one another before getting to bigger groups later in the year.	*Create groups of three, and have two people converse while the third student takes notes on communication skills. Rotate roles so all three students get a chance to be observers. *Give points/credit for inviting more people into the conversation rather than dominating the conversation.
Technology	
Low Tech	*High Tech*
*Create a question box or question wall for students who want to clarify information or push thinking further. Encourage students to leave a question or take a question to answer.	*Have students post questions in a live feed via platforms such as https://www.pubble.io/live-qa

SAMPLE MATERIALS

Your Name:____

Nominate 2 students who added the most depth to the conversation and employed the most skills effectively.	Explanation to support your nominations.
1.	
2.	

Self-Evaluation

1. What overall skill do you think you most consistently demonstrated? Did you meet your speaking goals? Why or why not?
2. Do you feel that you should be nominated as one of the top speakers for today's discussion? Provide specific reasons as to why or why not.

Figure 3.1 Discussion Reflection. *Source*: Author created.

STRATEGY 12: SMALL GROUP STATIONS

Chapter Contributors
Rebecca Austern, PS 261 (NY), 1st grade
Mary Brady, Lloyd Memorial HS (KY), 10th and 12th grade

Groups of 3–5 students move through stations (work areas/centers) varied by content, skills development, and readiness. Students may work in homogeneous or heterogeneous groups. Each station provides chunked materials and activities that enable students to work on and develop specific Knowledge/Skills/Dispositions (KSD).

STRATEGY IMPLEMENTATION

1. *Determine the K/S/D You Want to Focus on for the Stations*—Consider how:
   - K/S/D correlate with standards and assessments
   - Learning experiences you are designing help students meet or exceed the unit objectives

Building a Culture of Collaboration

When students engage in group work, they are utilizing dispositions such as respect for others and for procedures that foster learning, openness to new ideas and thinking that differs from their own, consideration of conflicting ideas, and so much more! To support students' development of these dispositions, teachers and students work together to build a culture of collaboration.

2. *Preparing the Stations*—Decide which K/S/D you will focus on at each station and what students will specifically be doing at each station. Additionally, think about:
   - How you can vary the tasks at each station to enable students to develop the K/S/D in different ways
   - How you can arrange the location of stations for maximum focus (e.g., If a station might lead to students being a bit louder, this would go in a far corner of the room)
   - What materials you need for each station
3. *Determine Groups*—Selecting the optimal groups can make a big difference in having the stations run smoothly. When determining groups consider:
   - The type of grouping that is best (homogeneous vs. heterogeneous abilities, interest, student relationships)
   - Roles that students might take (if any) within the group

Notes about Roles

- All students should be held accountable for doing equitable amounts of work during the task (e.g., If a student is assigned a presenter or timekeeper role, that student would still be responsible for processes related to the K/S/D of the activity).
- Every person is challenged within their given role. Students may take on roles that align with their readiness or abilities, or they may take on roles that challenge them to grow in terms of their readiness or abilities.
- Groups of 3–5 people are often ideal because group members hold each other more accountable in smaller groups.
- Consider scaffolding the difficulty of assignments based on group abilities.
- Change who has responsibilities to push students who don't typically take on those responsibilities.

4. *Give Clear Instructions*—Effective instructions are critical to any activity. Great instructions should take into account:
   - The learning goals for the group stations
   - What students are expected to do at each station
   - The procedures for moving from station to station
   - How students collaborate with their group members and understand their roles within the group

Notes about Giving Instructions

1. Be prepared to provide instructions in *three ways:*
   a. Verbally
   b. Posted on the board/projector
   c. Individually for the students (handout or on the computer)
2. Be sure you have 100 percent attention before you give instructions.
3. Give full class instructions before students get into groups. This reduces chatter and "feedback" about groupings.
4. Model any elements of the work that you believe students may need to see and hear in order to understand.

5. *Dive In*—This is when students are completing the stations and you are circulating the room to support them. As you facilitate the small group stations, ask yourself:
   - Are students meeting the learning goals for their group stations?
   - What questions can I ask to support/extend their learning?
   - How are students managing challenges that arise?
   - How are they interacting with one another in ways that support learning and personal growth?
   - What unexpected learning/questions am I noting?

Teacher as Facilitator

**Time Checks*—Let students know how much time they have to complete their work at each station, and tell students roughly how far along they should be with their task at the time check.
**Smooth Transitions*—Determine the most efficient way for groups to transition from one station to the next.
**Shout-Outs*—Share examples of strong critical thinking, good questioning, positive interactions among group members.
**Check-Ins*—After students have completed two stations, bring the class together for 1 minute to get their feedback on how the process is going and any major takeaways they have from their work thus far. Reinforce the connection between their station work and K/S/D development.
**Whole Class Clarification*—If more than one group is struggling with an element of the stations, get the entire class's attention to reinforce or adapt instructions.
**Getting Back on Track*—If the class seems to be distracted from their station(s), pause to bring the class back together and reinforce the expectations and the reasoning behind each station in terms of K/S/D development.
**Conferencing*—Meet with students to determine their progress toward meeting objectives. You may pull individual students/groups to meet with you at your desk or you may join a group at their station to conference with them.
**Body Positioning*—Make sure as you circulate the room that you position your body in a way where you can always see the entire class, even if you are conferencing with a particular student or group.
**Get to Every Group*—When students start working, quickly check on each group to ensure they are good to begin and then take time checking in with and supporting each group as equitably as possible throughout the station work.

6. *Share and Reflect*—Once students have completed the stations, make time to have groups and students share what they learned, reflect on what they learned, and reflect on the process. Consider different approaches to sharing and reflecting:
    - *Sharing What Was Learned with One Another*—Do you want students to share as a whole group, doing a gallery walk, through Google Slides, or another way?
    - *Recording the Debrief/Reflection*—How should students take notes on new information/new perspectives they learn from their peers? Is there a graphic organizer or guided notes that can help with students' note taking?
    - *Assessing the Stations Process*—What information do you want to gather from students about their experiences during the small stations process? (e.g., Did the process enable students to develop the desired K/S/D from the stations? Are there elements of the stations process that need to be adapted in the future? If so, what and how?)

7. *Intentional Next Steps*—After completing your sharing and critical reflection, think about what the next steps are for you and your students. Consider:
    - Which students might be ready for a particular next step, reinforcement, or support.
    - Which future lessons might provide opportunities to reinforce the K/S/D further.

Variations on Station Movement and Placement

- Students remain at their seats and tasks get passed to them.
  - For older students, one assignment/project is handed out to each group that incorporates each station task.
  - The teacher chunks the timing for students.
- Students may work in the hall if you need more space.
- Play music during transitions from station to station.

How to Implement the Strategy at Varied Grade Levels

Elementary	*Middle*	*High*
*Link setting group norms for the stations with your class' discussions of community. Have students consider how they are contributing to the classroom community through their roles in their groups. *Consider shorter blocks of time for students at each station because younger students' attention spans are shorter.	*Spend additional time working on establishing group dynamics and individual roles within groups because middle schoolers are experiencing emotional and physical developmental changes that impact their interpersonal skills.	*Draw from students' experiences with small group work to determine best practices (e.g., students can help define and develop roles within the groups).

WHY I LIKE THIS STRATEGY

"Small group stations put learning in students' hands, encourage collaboration, support students' presentation skills, and instill pride in their own work. This strategy allows me to see where students are struggling specifically and provide support."

—*Mary Brady*

"I find that the students are able, with my guidance or proctoring, to begin to work together and build on each others' thinking more authentically than in 1:1 conferencing. They also begin to notice and learn from one another—try out what peers are doing, and compete—in a great way—to solve and progress together."

—*Rebecca Austern*

CONSIDERING DIFFERENT TYPES OF LEARNERS

Small group stations are a great strategy for:

1. *English Language Learners* (ELLs) because the materials can be adapted to suit their needs; in heterogeneous language groups, language development may be supported, and in homogeneous language groups, they may find comfort working with other ELLs.

2. *Special Education* students because scaffolding, differentiation, and supports are intentionally integrated into the stations and groupings by the teacher—whether a teacher decides to utilize heterogeneous or homogeneous groupings based on academic skills.
3. *Gifted and Talented* students because it allows for more challenging work rather than extra work.

> "The most impacted kids in these types of activities are my low self-confidence ones . . . the kids who will never raise their hands during whole-class instruction. Two of these students were easy to cry if they were put on the spot or felt they didn't know what to do. Using these stations, those two kids in particular had the brightest eyes and offered to share the most frequently."
>
> —*Rebecca Austern*

Adaptation for Different Assets/Needs

Cultural Diversity	
Limited Diversity	*Lots of Diversity*
*Though your class might not be very culturally diverse, students can be exposed to different cultures outside of school through media, travel, and other experiences. Within the stations, find ways to draw from this knowledge to broaden students' views and engage in conversations that explore and celebrate differences. *Integrate content at the stations that both aligns with the cultural backgrounds of your students in the class and exposes students to new cultures. *Identify noncultural differences between your students (e.g., socioeconomic, fashion, neighborhood, sports allegiance, food interests, etc.) and find ways to share and celebrate those differences within the stations.	*Create groups based on *commonalities* (like if they speak a similar language other than English or family traditions). This will enable students to feel comfortable and supported by their peers to engage in challenging work at the stations. OR *Create groups where there is a *diversity of cultural backgrounds* represented in each group. When this happens, the stations should be designed to engage students in tasks and dialogue that allow each student to share their own backgrounds and experiences and learn from their group members. *Integrate content at the stations that both aligns with the cultural backgrounds of your students in the class and exposes students to new cultures. *Find ways to embed the day's or unit's identified skills and dispositions into each station when the content/knowledge for the stations is culturally responsive (e.g., one station might be focused on the skills of problem solving and analyzing primary source texts by learning about Dominican civil rights leaders).

(*Continued*)

Adaptation for Different Assets/Needs (Continued)

Academic K/S/D Diversity	
Limited Diversity	*Limited Diversity*
*Vary how you form groups. Though a class may generally be homogeneous in academic makeup, you will still see specific K/S/D that students need to develop, so you can group accordingly. *Create groups based on interest (rather than skill). At the elementary level, you could do Pokemon math, pet math, etc. At the middle school/high school level, you could group according to themes related to after-school activities such as sports, music, art, etc. *Remember, you may want to keep groups the same at first so students can work on developing their group work dispositions; over time, you will want to vary the construct of the groups. (See roles described in *Strategy in Action: Establishing Routines by Using Base Groups* on page 14 for ideas about supporting collaboration.)	*Keep the K/S/D that you want students to develop consistent while differentiating the content, process, and product based on students' readiness, interest, and learning modality (e.g., if students are analyzing language in a text, you may provide quotes for some students and have others find the passages they want to analyze themselves). *Vary how you form groups. Form groups of students according to *homogeneous* levels of K/S/D. This may allow for students to work at a pace that is appropriate for them. OR *Form *heterogeneous* groups to allow students to collaborate with one another and find ways to work through processes based on their different strengths and areas for growth. This is important for supporting dispositional development; students learn how to take on responsibilities and balance work with others. *Remember, you may want to keep groups the same at first so students can work on developing their group work dispositions; over time, you will want to mix up the groups.

SAMPLE MATERIALS

The following organizers (Figure 3.2) are meant to serve as general starting points for helping students reflect on their learning at the stations and to respond to one another after completing the stations. Consider how you might adapt this organizer to best meet your content area objectives and your students' needs. Additional organizers would likely need to be created for use *at each station* in alignment with the activity's K/S/D objectives.

Small Group Stations Sharing and Reflection

Directions:

Step 1 - Based on your work at each station, jot down the big ideas that you learn and any questions that arise.
Step 2 - Share your work with the other groups and give each other feedback.
Step 3 - Jot down any new ideas/affirmations that result from peer feedback.

Station	Big Ideas	Questions	New Ideas/ Affirmations from Peer Feedback

Group Station Work Self-Assessment

Directions:

Step 1 - Before you begin your station work, review and list the Knowledge, Skills, and Dispositions objectives for this station work.
Step 2 - After completing the stations, reflect and write about how you met or exceeded the Knowledge, Skills, and Dispositions objectives for the station work.

Objectives	Evidence
Knowledge Objectives	Evidence of Meeting or Exceeding *Knowledge* Objectives:
Skills Objectives	Evidence of Meeting or Exceeding *Skills* Objectives:
Dispositions Objectives	Evidence of Meeting or Exceeding *Dispositions* Objectives:

Figure 3.2 Group Stations Reflection and Self-Assessment. *Source*: Author created.

STRATEGY 13: ARTS INTEGRATION

Chapter Contributors
Emilio Burgos, PS 360 Queens (NY), Kindergarten–3rd grade
Bette Sloane, Mineola HS (NY), 8th–12th grade

Arts Integration is the incorporation of music, visual arts, and/or movement to enhance what happens in the classroom. For instance, you can make transitions more fun by using music to serve as signals to move to new activities and deepen learning by engaging students in transfer of understanding among different art media. All of this involves opportunities to model risk-taking for your students.

STRATEGY IMPLEMENTATION

1. *Let Go of Your Self-Doubt and Judgment*—Incorporating the arts into your instruction can be a step outside of your comfort zone. If this is the case, before you actually bring this approach into the classroom, you need to let go of your worries:
   - Decide which artistic medium to incorporate.
   - Let students know that this is something new that you are all going to try together.

2. *Determine HOW You Want to Incorporate the Arts into Your Classroom*—Will you connect the arts with routines and transitions or integrate them into class instruction?
   - *Music for Routines and Transitions*—A great way to start with arts integration is by using music as a cue for classroom routines. Music can set the tone for what is coming next.
     - Use quiet, fluid music to prepare students for working silently, calmly, and staying focused.
     - Use rhythmic and beating music for packing up or lining up.
     - Use popular songs to get students excited about an event or visit.
     - Create a classroom playlist based on each student's favorite songs.

> A Note about Vulnerability
>
> In her TED Talk, *Listening to Shame*, Brené Brown says, "Vulnerability is not weakness. I define vulnerability as emotional risk, exposure, uncertainty. It fuels our daily lives . . . vulnerability is our most accurate measure of courage."
>
> When you take risks with incorporating the arts in your classroom, you are vulnerable because you are doing something out of the norm; you are likely going to raise the energy level of your students, and some may see this as chaotic; you are trying to make connections that may not initially be clear. Acting courageously, taking these risks is important to model for students. Be as overt as you can about what you are doing, why you are doing it, and any need for support or understanding from your students.
>
> "You need to have trust in yourself and in your students. Singing, dancing, and dramatic reading gets silly, but that is OK because there is a reason for it."
>
> —*Emilio Burgos*

- *Movement for Routines and Transitions*—Another powerful way to integrate arts into classroom routines is through movement.
  - Have a fun dance before a test for students to release stress.
  - Incorporate yoga between activities for stress relief.
  - Give students the opportunity to lead stretch breaks.
- *Visual Arts Classroom Instruction*—Incorporating visual arts into instruction can enhance students' content area knowledge and skills and can support interdisciplinary learning. Some examples include:
  - *Turning Narratives into Classroom Comic Strips*—Take any class text and break it up into parts (could be one sentence per student or multiple sentences per student). Then have each student convert their assigned sentence(s) into an image with a caption. Next, put all of the students' creations together to create one large class comic strip that represents the text.
  - *Drawing Punctuation*—Represent through drawing how punctuations help fluency. Water colors represent commas (a smooth pause and a light amount of "break" in our words); crayons represent periods (a definitive stamp); markers represent exclamation points (rich in color and expression).
  - *Critiquing Visual Art*—Use a photograph or piece of art for your students to critique. You can use graphic organizers to support the analysis and evaluation process, and then compare this process to critical thinking about class texts. See Figure 3.3.
- *Drama for Classroom Instruction*—Drama can increase reading fluency and comprehension. Through drama, you can:
  - Model expressive reading.
  - Listen or view plays that relate to content.

> "Reading 'fluently' or with expression is simply acting the words to bring the story to life."
>
> —*Emilio Burgos*

3. *Model Thinking Processes and Language*—Make your thinking about the connections between art and Knowledge/Skills/Dispositions (KSD) overt:
   - When using art to connect with classroom routines, explain why you chose the song, movement, or visual to be connected with that routine.
   - When integrating art into the curriculum, be overt about the connections that you see. This will help students to explain their connections and to bridge the K/S/D they are developing among varied content areas.
   - Consider questions that you can ask to support and extend students' thinking.

> Talk the Talk!
> Teach the language that your students need in order to discuss art critically. Keywords that help articulate thinking are as follows:
> - Perspective
> - Tone
> - Detail
> - Composition
> - Contrast
>
> "The only thing you can't say is 'that's not art!' Who are we to judge this?"
>
> —*Bette Sloane*

4. *Invite Student Choice*—Students are a great source of inspiration and content when it comes to arts integration. Invite them to:
   - Suggest options for arts integration in routines (e.g., music for transitions).
   - Submit examples of art that relate to the K/S/D that you are teaching.

Students Need the Arts!

In his book, *The Element*, Ken Robinson (2009) writes, "Too many students pass through education and have their natural talents marginalized or ignored. The arts, sciences, humanities, physical education, languages, and math all have equal and central contributions to make to a student's education" (p. 247).

It is important to experience ideas, concepts, skills, and emotions through different media in order to process and generate new thinking.

CONSIDERING DIFFERENT TYPES OF LEARNERS

Arts integration is a great strategy for:

1. *English Language Learners* because this approach goes beyond language. If you can get a student to show what they know through art, they may demonstrate an understanding that is deeper than what they could show through writing or speaking in English.
2. *Special Education* students because it provides clear cues for classroom routines and expectations.
3. *Gifted and Talented* students because it creates opportunities for students to follow their artistic interests when extending their learning. This allows for more challenging work rather than extra work.

WHY I LIKE THIS STRATEGY

"Students know that when the alphabet song comes on they need their phonics books and a pencil and should be sitting on the rug by the letter Z ready to work. The music within transitions minimizes my hand on their independence and allows them to be the 'rulers of their time.'"

—*Emilio Burgos*

"I always think of photography as a primary source. It's so accessible now. Most high school students have access to a camera phone or iPad, so photography has become a constant in their lives. . . . I like helping them to think critically about this medium that surrounds them and understand the connections between what they are learning and what they are seeing."

—*Bette Sloane*

How to Implement the Strategy at Varied Grade Levels

Elementary	*Middle*	*High*
*Connect arts through classroom routines first so students get used to seeing, hearing, and moving in creative ways.	*Model how you struggle through possible discomfort in thinking about the arts and stress the idea that there are no "wrong" answers.	*Increase student input into the types of arts that are integrated into routines and curricular connections.

Adaptation for Different Assets/Needs

Timing	
Limited Time	*Lots of Time*
*Use Arts Integration to support classroom routines. Knowing the cues from music or visuals will help you save time in the classroom.	*Dedicate time to developing patterns of approaches so students have the opportunity to make the connections clear between the arts and the related learning of K/S/D.
Arts Exposure	
Limited Arts Exposure	*Lots of Arts Exposure*
*Some students have very little exposure to the arts. Students can be nervous to talk about art in the classroom. They don't want to sound "stupid." Get them comfortable with the idea that there is often more than one right answer. Remind them that no observation is too small.	*Keep the K/S/D that you want students to develop consistent while differentiating the content based on students' readiness and interests. Students may apply their knowledge of the arts to helping you determine the connections that they can make and the media to use in relation to routines and activities.

STRATEGY IN ACTION: A PICTURE IS WORTH A THOUSAND WORDS IN MATH

"One of my first years teaching, I was explaining the importance of parallel lines. I could see my 9th grade geometry students' eyes start to glaze over. So, I told them, matter-of-factly, that our entire civilization is based on parallel lines. They, of course, thought I was using hyperbole. I was not. I started asking them how things would work without parallel lines. How would stairs work? How would floors and ceilings and walls stand up? How would the lines on the road work? Where would we drive? The students started looking all over the room and calling out parallel lines: the windows, the board, the tiles, the door, the lights, the desk legs, the bricks *in* the walls. I asked them to ponder how many examples of parallel lines they interact with on a daily basis, if that is only what they could see in this one room. I immediately offered them an opportunity to photograph these examples for extra credit. I was blown away by their photographs. I set up a gallery in the front-of-school showcase and the project grew from there. My favorite part of telling classes about the assignment is seeing certain students light up when I say in a math class 'ok, we're going to do an art project.'"

—*Bette Sloane*

SAMPLE MATERIALS

ANALYZING ART

What stands out in this artwork?
Is something very large? Placed in the center? Very colorful?

What stands out to you after looking at this artwork a bit longer?
What details did you notice after looking with a careful eye? What might a person not see at first?

What senses does this artwork stimulate?
Can you almost feel a breeze or smell something that is represented? Consider sight, smell, touch, taste, sound.

What colors does the artist use?
Are the colors cool or warm? Bright or soft? If the artwork is black and white, where are there shadows or brighter parts?

What style does the artist use?
Is this realistic or abstract? Are there interesting brush strokes or color patterns or visual manipulations?

RESPONDING TO ART

What does this artwork make you *feel*?
What details bring on these feelings? How might your feelings compare with the feelings of others? If this artwork was created in a different time period, how might your feelings compare with those of viewers from the past?

What does this artwork make you *think* about?
What details bring on these thoughts? How might your thoughts compare with the thoughts of others? If this artwork was created in a different time period, how might your thoughts compare with those of viewers from the past?

Figure 3.3 Analyzing Art. *Source*: Author created.

STRATEGY 14: MOCK TRIALS

Chapter Contributors
Sarah Gibson, MS 88 (NY), 7th grade
Amaris Rodriguez Brown, RFK HS (NY), 11th and 12th grade

Mock Trials include a range of students' skills, but primarily focuses on the use of content-based evidence integrated with role play presentation. During the mock trial, students take on assigned roles and work their way through the stages of a trial, from evidence gathering through the trial itself. Placing students in teams on different sides of a given scenario challenges students to: work collaboratively; develop research, analytical, and questioning skills; work with evidence, evaluation, and supporting claims; enhance public speaking; and address and work with multiple perspectives. Additionally, mock trials introduce students to different career paths within the justice system and help make connections between content learning and our greater society more overt. This strategy enlivens a typical classroom setting by engaging in friendly competition and acting.

STRATEGY IMPLEMENTATION

Part I: Teacher Preparation

You must prepare extensively by selecting the best possible topic, defining and breaking down tasks and roles for the trial, and creating rubrics that align with those roles and tasks.

1. *Determine a Debatable/Controversial Topic*—Select a topic related to your content that can foster opposing viewpoints or multiple perspectives and that does not have a clear-cut answer.
   - Make a list of possible debatable/controversial topics that work within the context of your unit.
   - Look at possible background information, primary and secondary sources, precedent court cases, and other materials for each possible topic.
   - Go with the topic that provides the greatest and most well-balanced amount of supporting materials.

2. *Define and Break Down Tasks for Roles in the Trial*—Based on the topic you select, determine:
   - *Roles*—What roles are necessary to have an effective, balanced, engaging trial?

Typical Roles in a Mock Trial

- Prosecuting Attorneys
- Defense Attorneys
- Legal Counsel (Prosecution and Defense)
- Witnesses (Prosecution and Defense)
- Judge(s)
- Jury

- *Timing for the Trial*—How long will you spend on the trial (preparation and trial)?
- *Number of Tasks*—How many tasks are feasible for each role based on the timing?
- *Differentiating Tasks*—Break down concrete tasks for each role that include:
  - The details and steps for each task
  - When that task is due
  - How each task will be assessed/given feedback

3. *Create a Rubric for Each Role*—Create specific rubrics for each role within the trial that include preparation, performance tasks, collaboration, and reflection.

Part II: Student Preparation

Once you have set up the foundation for the mock trial, begin the process of engaging the students in the process and product.

1. *Research the Topic (All Sides)*—Before students are assigned roles for the mock trial, introduce the mock trial topic and its multiple sides. Then have *all students* research *all sides* of the topic so each student is prepared to take on any role on any side of the mock trial. Research steps might include:
   - Locate and develop historical evidence and materials that surround the chosen topic, and set these materials up so that students can explore, research, and collect evidence on different claims related to the topic. As you finalize materials, consider: reading level, depth and rigor of materials, and scaffolding steps needed in the design process.
   - Determine: (1) how students will interact with the material, (2) whether it will be solely developed and curated by you, and (3) if students will engage in the research process on their own or if students will work in groups or pairs.

Different Research Options

All research options should include students recording their findings using graphic organizers.

Teacher-Generated

- Stations with different types of evidence (primary/secondary), through different types of media (articles, websites, videos) that are representative of all perspectives (See *Strategy 12: Small Group Stations* on page 75).

- Article analysis with guided questions
- WebQuests and Videos

Student-Generated

- Use the library resources to uncover information on different sides of the topic.
- Use search engines with "key word" searches to evaluate reliable sources and determine useful information on the different sides of the topic.
- Interview experts on the topic.
- Survey classmates to gather public opinion.

2. *Determine Teams and Roles*—Once students have gathered background information and evidence on the topic, review the objective of the mock trial, what the parts of the trial will include, and what the different roles are. Then, students will be assigned to a team (Prosecution or Defense) and roles within those teams. When selecting teams and roles, consider the following:
   - *Selecting Teams*—Try to select teams that have students who both complement and challenge one another. To do this:
     - Let students submit a list of students they want to work with and those they would prefer not to work with. (See the *Strategy in Action: Establishing Routines by Using Base Groups* example on page 14 from *Strategy 2: Establishing Routines.*)
     - Assign *struggling students* to the side/team that is most comfortable for them.
     - Assign *accelerated students* to the side/team that is most challenging for them.
     - Build in tasks where students can develop independent skills as well as team leadership skills.
   - *Choosing Roles*—Like with selecting teams, you can consider letting students have a say in their roles or assign roles for students. Ensure students are supported in effectively carrying out whichever role they are assigned (see "Typical Roles" above).

REMEMBER: All students should have roles that require the same level of effort and amount of time to complete; however, those tasks will differ based on the skills, strengths, and areas of growth for each student.

3. *Prepare for the Role*—Students take the designated amount of time to prepare for their role based on their role's assigned tasks.
   - *Timing*—The tasks for each role should be chunked with concrete amounts of time assigned to each task to help students pace their preparation.
   - *Collaboration*—Require that students give feedback to one another before finalizing their individual tasks. Some roles and tasks will rely on sharing and collaborating more than others (e.g., defense witnesses working with defense attorneys to prepare for questioning and cross-examination).
   - *Preparing for Your Side*—Students should first prepare for their side of the argument (gather evidence, look at precedent cases if relevant to your topic, write opening and closing statements, prepare questions and answers, develop a witness script, etc.).

- *Prepare for the Other Side*—Next, students should prepare for the other side (review evidence that supports their side, creating cross-examination questions for their witnesses, consider questions your witnesses will be asked, and anticipated answers for all questions, etc.).

4. *Judge and Jury Selection*—To keep *all students* focused on researching both sides in depth, consider inviting a guest judge and jury to join you for the trial or delaying judge and jury selection until the day of (or before) the trial. If students in the class are going to serve as judge and jury, consider:
   - *Who to Select*—Select students who will not significantly take away from the product of either the prosecution or defense (e.g., don't take away witnesses who have prepared specifically for that role). This also means you need to assign multiple people to each role on the legal teams, so when a few of those individuals are called to serve as judge or jury, the other team members will be equipped to perform well.
   - *Preparation for New Roles*—Provide graphic organizers that help students prepare for their new role as either a judge or jury member and give them concrete guidance on what they need to do and complete during the trial. While the new judge and jury prepare for their roles, legal teams will review their tasks and figure out how to fill gaps of individuals they lost.

5. *Trial Run-Through*—Before starting the trial:
   - Review the process and steps of the trial.
   - Have each legal team do a run-through of their parts of the trial so they (and you) can give feedback to one another and make last-minute changes.
6. *Conduct the Mock Trial*—This is the fun part! Things to remember during the trial:
   - *Every student* has a task during *each part* of the trial so each student is actively involved.
   - The *teacher* provides informal notes/feedback for each student's performance task.
   - Ensure the *jury* is reminded to come to a *decision based on evidence* and not their personal opinions or their previous roles on one team or the other. (Jurors' grades should be aligned with these expectations and tied to the graphic organizer given to jurors to record their findings during the trial.)
7. *Reflect on the Experience*—After the jury verdict, give students time to reflect on their process and the task overall. Ground reflections in the students' individual/team rubrics.

CONSIDERING DIFFERENT TYPES OF LEARNERS

Mock Trials can be adapted for different types of learners:

1. *English Language Learners* can use a glossary of legal and other relevant terms while being assigned roles that are more scripted with translation.
2. *Special Education* students can receive additional scaffolding, differentiation, and supports that enable them to thrive in their assigned roles.
3. *Gifted and Talented* students can be given the most complex roles/arguments within the trial.

STRATEGY IN ACTION: A MIDDLE SCHOOL BOSTON MASSACRE MOCK TRIAL

"Mock Trial is an activity I have set aside one week for each year. We conduct a trial around the Boston Massacre. It is an engaging topic for 7th graders as there are a wealth of resources out there from the actual trial transcripts to the great film reenactments from a series like HBO's John Adams. One of the aspects that takes a bit of time for this class project is the introductory research students complete. They research documents in stations as a team. They read excerpts, analyze images, consider the idea of propaganda, before they establish which claim they will need to argue at the trial (Murder or Self-Defense). After the research phase, students are given their roles, specifically witness, lawyer (Prosecution, Defense) and jury members. Students take some time to prepare, particularly witnesses and their legal team. The jury members use this time to investigate aspects of court verdicts, ideas about jury, and different types of courts. The day of the trial is fun to watch particularly because of the students' portrayal of various witnesses and the legal teams' efforts to cross examine the prepared witnesses. For this performance task I typically assign the more shy students the role of witness so that they are pushed to participate more, as it is a mid-year assessment. The more confident speakers and strong questioners tend to shine in the role of legal team, but they can be supported by quieter studious students who have organized their team's research evidence. The jury members practice rating an argument and look beyond their own bias, both for the event and for their peers. At the culmination of the trial they deliberate in the hall and come back to brief the class on their decision."

—*Sarah Gibson*

How to Implement the Strategy at Varied Grade Levels

Elementary	*Middle*	*High*
*Choose a topic that is fun and engaging for the students. *Provide all resources students need, at appropriate Lexile levels, to learn about their topic and simple graphic organizers to record their information. *Spend extra days on building your students' research and analysis skills. *Show students clips of entertaining trials where you can highlight the different roles in trials for students to emulate. *Create fill-in-the-blank scripts where students can fill in the evidence they found. *Dress up!	*Choose a topic that is both fun, but that also does not have an easy answer. *Integrate more primary than secondary sources into the materials students are analyzing. *Use more detailed graphic organizers. *Work on developing research skills (print and digital). *Provide graphic organizers with guiding questions for students' preparation tasks. *Dress up!	*Choose a topic that has multiple perspectives and requires deep analysis. *Have students research and discover materials relevant to the trial rather than providing them with most of the resources. *Provide a loose structure for the trial, but put students in charge of developing most of the materials, evidence, and scripts necessary for their side to win the trial. *Dress up!

WHY I LIKE THIS STRATEGY

"Mock Trials force students to use more real-world skills and you can infuse multiple modes of learning into these types of tasks and assessments. These are the types of team projects that I feel engage students as well as create competitive and fun environments for learning. Students really look forward to these types of events in the classroom to the extent that they dress up or bring artifact evidence. It makes the routine of school change, and that is constantly needed at the middle school age. Through a deeper engagement in learning students improve their historical argumentative, analysis, and public speaking skills, as well as building on improved teamwork."

—Sarah Gibson

STRATEGY IN ACTION: MOCK TRIAL IN A HIGH SCHOOL SCIENCE CLASS

"When the students took on the challenge of preparing for and taking part in a mock murder trial in which the defendant based his defense on an MAOA-L gene variant that impacted his decision-making, I got to see them take true ownership of something. I didn't give them any rules for serving as the defense or prosecution. Students for each legal team became leaders and delegated roles. It was interesting and heartening to watch how the group dynamics were formed. I didn't even state that the jury needed a foreman. Rather the group came up with the idea that they needed a person in this role and elected a student. The kids just ran with this. They took this seriously and wanted to make a strong case. Some even dressed up for their parts.

The prosecution and defense really had to prepare because there was an element of surprise. The groups did not know who the other side would call. Each side had 15 minutes to present their case. Then they got to cross-examine the other witnesses. The witnesses also had to prepare well because they did not know for sure what they would be asked by the opposing side. The student who played the man who was accused of killing his wife struggled in class, and his team coaxed him and helped him along. He had a 'go to' line: saying 'this just isn't in my character.' It fit the role well, and gave him time to think.

Overall, this project was powerful for the students because it put so much of the learning in their hands. They had to think about what details would help them build their case and connect scientific evidence with constructing an argument and operating within the expectations of the legal system. For me, this project was powerful because I was able to let go of my role as instructor and move into the role of facilitator of learning."

—Amaris Rodriguez Brown

Adaptation for Different Assets/Needs

Student Dispositions	
Quiet Students *Assign roles that will enable quiet students to thrive while also pushing them outside their comfort zone with the right supports (e.g., guiding questions they can answer and then read aloud or pairing them with more talkative students who they get along with that will challenge them to be more vocal).	*Talkative Students* *These students may want to take on larger roles in the trial (lawyer, key witness, jury foreman). It may also be helpful for more talkative students to coach/encourage the quieter students who take on roles that are a stretch for them. *During trial preparation, give points/credit for inviting more people into the conversation rather than dominating the conversation.
Class Size	
Small Class *Reduce the number of roles to only key roles necessary for the trial (few prosecutors and defense attorneys, one judge, and fewer jurors). *Allow students to take on more responsibilities with their roles (if appropriate). *Give more one-on-one and small group support.	*Large Class* *Create more roles that ensure all students have a productive task to take on. That includes creating roles like journalists, extra witnesses, fact checkers, larger juries, etc. *Select a topic that is more complex and will require the larger teams to use the additional members to uncover and analyze evidence to support their side of the topic. *Have groups submit work that you can give feedback on the next day (if not enough time to meet with everyone during class).

SAMPLE MATERIALS

Roles for Our Mock Trial

Each of you will play a role in our mock trial. This role will change the next time you participate in a mock trial.

Roles	What do you need to do? (Job)
Defense Lawyers	Your job is to present your team's strongest evidence to the class. You will meet with your legal team to prepare at least four strong pieces of evidence to present. You must decide who (which lawyer) will present which evidence. (You don't want to repeat information during the trial.)
Legal Counsel *Assistants to Lawyer*	Your job is to help the lawyers. You are offering support and advice about what they should say and how to say it. They will practice it with you first. Give them strong feedback. You can also, if you choose, present some of the evidence during the trial.
Prosecution *Cross Examination= Crossfire*	Your job is to take charge during cross examination or CROSSFIRE. After your opponents have presented their evidence your side will have an opportunity to expose the weaknesses of their argument or "Stump" them by asking them QUESTIONS. You will need to direct your questions to the team and think on your feet to create them while they present their case.
Jury Member	Your job is to judge the quality and presentation of the evidence presented on both sides. You need to be unbiased, that means you need to judge the case not based on what you already think, but what is being presented by both sides. You will take notes on each side when they present and compare your notes with the other jury members. At the end of the case you will deliberate (discuss) and decide as a team whose argument was stronger.

Figure 3.4 Mock Trial Roles. *Source*: Sarah Gibson.

Mock Trial Protocol

Our mock trial will start with a draw to decide who will defend their position first.

1. *SIDE A:* Lawyer reads *OPENING STATEMENT:* Introduces team claim and gives some background information about the topic in debate.

2. *SIDE A:* Lawyer introduces *EVIDENCE* to the court. Evidence presented must be ranked and detailed and organized so it's easy for the JURY to follow. You must present at least 4 evidence examples about the topic, include reasoning in your examples.

3. Then comes *CROSSFIRE.* This is the opportunity for the other team (Team B) to question the evidence presented by (Team A). The goal is to "stump" the team or make the team appear their evidence is weak. The only people that can ask questions during this CROSSFIRE are *Team B's Prosecution Team.*

4. SIDE B: Lawyer Reads *OPENING STATEMENT:* Introduces team claim and gives Background information about the topic in debate.

5. *SIDE A:* Lawyer introduces *EVIDENCE* to court. Evidence presented must be ranked and detailed and organized so it's easy for the JURY to follow. You must present at least 4 evidence examples about the topic;; include reasoning in your examples.

6. Then comes *CROSSFIRE* again, but reversed. (Team A) *Team A's Prosecution Team* gets to question (Team B) on their evidence with the goal of "stumping" them.

7. *JURY DELIBERATION:* The Jury will discuss privately their ruling on the effectiveness of each team's argument.

LAWYER'S OPENING STATEMENT FRAME

DIRECTIONS: Use this frame to develop your opening statement. Make sure to highlight the most powerful elements of your case!

Ladies and gentlemen of the jury, today you will hear why ________________
The case we will share with today will prove _______________________.
First of all, _______________________.
Our first piece of evidence supports this case because _____________________
The experts we will call include ____________________________.
These experts are important because _______________________.
We know for a fact that ________________________________.
According to research, we know _______________________________.

LAWYERS' QUESTION STARTERS

DIRECTIONS: Use these starters to stump the other side! Make sure you ask clear questions.

In your team's statements, you mentioned this evidence__________. Could you explain more about ____________?
What did you mean when you stated ____________? OR Could you restate _______?
Is there anything else you can say about ________________?
I have a question that relates to _________________.
We want to know what your team thinks about ___________.
How can you say _______________ if ___________?
What if __________? What would happen if ____________?

Figure 3.4 (Continued)

JURY MEMBER NOTES

Step 1: With your Jury Members, discuss the following question:

As a Jury Member, why is it important that you remain IMPARTIAL (fair) and OPEN-MINDED as you listen to the evidence of this case. Why should you hear all the evidence before you make a judgement about which case is stronger? Why does it matter in real life too?

Step 2: With your Jury Members, discuss the following questions:

What knowledge do you already have about this topic? In what ways might it sway your thinking? How can you be sure that you will remain impartial?
Complete the Case Notes Table as you hear both sides of the debate. Check off with an X the ranked scores for each side. You must rank each category from 4, 3, 2, 1. (Highest to lowest)

Which Side Presented a Stronger Case?

Step 3: In your Jury Deliberation… Discuss with the JURY your opinion about which side presented a better argument by using your rankings organizers. You must all agree, so find out how to make a compromise. You might try taking a public vote. When you make it official, complete the following statement below…

After hearing both defense arguments in this trial, we, the Jury, find that the ________________________ argued a stronger Case. We feel this way because….

Side A: Claim: ____

JURY FOCUS AREAS	1 Ineffective	2 Developing	3 Effective	4 Highly Effective
Lawyers presented evidence in a clear and focused way. I could understand most of the ideas that were shared. Lawyers made an effort to be professional and persuasive. Notes:				
Evidence was specific and applied to the team's claim. Ideas shared related to the claim and reasoning was given to explain the evidence presented. Team seemed well researched and prepared. Notes:				
During Crossfire, lawyers presented strong questions to the other team. Questions asked were clear and seemed strong enough to "stump" the other team. Notes:				

REPEAT FOR SIDE B.

Figure 3.4 (Continued)

STRATEGY 15: STUDENT SELF-ASSESSMENT

Chapter Contributors
Katherine O'Sullivan, Bay Shore Middle School (NY), 7th grade
Rachel Field Dennis, Morris Academy for Collaborative Studies (NY), 12th grade

Students consider how their knowledge, skills, and confidence in learning have evolved and what they still need to do to make progress. Self-assessment can be verbal or nonverbal and is most effective when it is based on clear criteria. It can take place before beginning a new topic to determine students' readiness, during a lesson for students to check-in on their engagement in the process, or after a lesson to determine students' understanding and reflect on their actions.

STRATEGY IMPLEMENTATION

1. *Create Your Self-Assessment System*—Self-assessment can take many forms:
   - *Spoken*—Discuss the learning process and level of understanding in student pairs, small groups, teacher-student conferences, or as a class. In addition to directly discussing the content, you can engage students in a metacognitive discussion about their learning. Ask questions such as:
     - What new understandings did you develop today?
     - What more do you want to learn?
     - What skills did you use today?
     - How confident do you feel using these skills?
     - How did you work through difficulty?
     - How did you celebrate success?
   - *Written*—Students use a scorecard (see Figure 3.5) to reflect on their engagement in the activity and their understanding of the content.
   - *Visual*—Students hold up emojis or different colored flags to represent levels of understanding or feelings of confidence with the content/skills (See *Strategy in Action: Emojis*).
   - *Kinesthetic*—Thumbs up for full understanding, thumbs sideways for partial understanding, thumbs down for little to no understanding.

> Once Is Not Enough!
>
> "You have to use the system you choose multiple times, otherwise the students don't buy-in."
>
> —*Rachel Field Dennis*

2. *Model the Process*—Demonstrate what you would like to see from students. Modeling self-assessment can take many forms:
   - *Fishbowl*—Students sit in a circle around you and a co-teacher or a student who has rehearsed with you. Carry out a discussion of the learning process, content learned, and skills developed. Ask the students in the outside circle to focus on what was said and how each of the speakers in the center responded to and pushed each other's thinking.
   - *Think-Aloud*—This works well with a scorecard or set of self-assessment reflection questions. Share the thinking that leads up to each of your answers to the questions.

- *Reboot*—As a class or in small groups, review the scorecard or self-assessment guide questions for reflection and determine possible answers that could lead to deeper learning. Give students a chance to "reboot" the scorecard or self-assessment questions by changing or adding to them.

3. *Do the Work*—Determine when in the learning process you want students to self-assess. This can happen more than once. Students may write, discuss, or even simply have hand signals (thumbs up, down, sideways) to represent responses to guiding questions like those listed below:
   - *Beginning*—How ready do you feel to do this work? Do you have any clarifying questions about the content, process, expectations?
   - *During*—How well are you understanding the content? What skills are you using to be successful? How are you working productively with your group/partner?
   - *After*—How well do you understand the content? Did you use skills effectively? How well did you work with others? What more do you need to understand or know how to do in order to be confident in your learning?

STOP, SELF-ASSESS, AND LISTEN!

REMEMBER! It is helpful to self-assess *during* the process because when a misconception arises with multiple students, the teacher can stop the class to clarify.

4. *Analyze Results*—Use students' self-assessments to determine what to do next. With your students, ask:
   - What content needs clarifying?
   - What skills need to be further developed?
   - What dispositions need refining?
5. *Determine Next Steps*—Based on what you and your students decide, provide next steps such as:
   - Full-class instruction
   - Access to video links for individuals who need to strengthen specific skills
   - Extra help with the teacher
   - Connecting with a learning buddy

CONSIDERING DIFFERENT TYPES OF LEARNERS

Student self-assessment is a great strategy for:

1. *English Language Learners* because they can use varying levels of language or simple images.
2. *Special Education* students because it provides clear expectations and allows for an individual rate of progression toward those expectations.
3. *Gifted and Talented* students because it creates opportunities for students to consider how best to work through challenges, and thus, progress to their individual level of accomplishment.

WHY I LIKE THIS STRATEGY

"Using self-assessment allows me to remove a heavy teacher voice in the classroom and opens the opportunity for students to lead discussions about their learning."

—*Rachel Field Dennis*

"Student self-assessment is important for finding an emotional and academic readiness starting point, and it enables students to self-direct their learning rather than being told by an authority what to do next."

—*Katherine O'Sullivan*

How to Implement the Strategy at Varied Grade Levels

Elementary	*Middle*	*High*
*Use emojis and color coding for students who do not yet have the reading and writing skills to complete more detailed self-assessment. Keep the prompts simple and focused on concrete objectives related to Knowledge/Skills/Dispositions development.	*Students create their own self-assessment guide after using a teacher- generated guide. You will know it is time to transition to student-generated self-assessments once they realize they have specific things they need to focus on (that other students might not need to).	*Increase metacognitive discussion of learning. This is the age at which students need to be thinking about what helps them make the most out of their learning experiences. Challenge students to develop a learning profile for themselves that outlines how they learn best (independently, in groups, through reading, listening, viewing, etc.). This will be important for students as they enter college and the workforce.

Adaptation for Different Assets/Needs

Timing	
Not a Lot of Time	*Lots of Time*
*Have students reflect by leaving a sticky note on the door as they exit. This might simply include: Name________________ I score my *understanding* as _________ because_________________________.	*The more time you have, the more often you can engage students in self-reflection. This allows for utilizing varied forms of self-reflection, and thus, can help students find forms of reflection that work best for them.
Technology	
Low Tech	*High Tech*
*Create a large-scale survey on the wall. Each day, students can place a sticker or post it with their initials to show how they self-assessed their understanding, skills, and/or participation. This will give students a sense of their progression over the course of the week. See Figure 3.5. *(see sample at end of chapter)	*Create an online survey for students to rank their understanding, skills, and/or participation. Over time, they can see how their self-assessment progresses by looking at a graph of their scores. *Use QR codes through the Plickers website to quickly gather data from students. You can adapt the questions on the scorecard and scan the room to get individual feedback.

STRATEGY IN ACTION: EMOJIS

"On the first day of school, I ask students to show me how they feel about math by creating an emoji and a 'text' sentence that shows their feelings. Students' responses range from crying face emojis to indifferent faces to angry faces to hearts. This brings out more than just their feelings about math. It also gives me insight into their personalities and who they are as students. Some are extremely open about their worries or their frustrations while others may be trying to please me with their response. We create a bulletin board in our classroom using these emojis and texts. In response to students who share negative emotions about math, I challenge them to find at least one thing they like about math through their work in our class. This gives me an opportunity to get students past their deficit thinking and worries about some of the base skills they may be lacking because I give them supports (a calculator) to move into mathematical thinking rather than computational skills. Throughout the year, students can share emojis to let me know how they are feeling about what we are working on. Based on those emojis that represent some frustration or confusion, I know who needs support."

—*Katherine O'Sullivan*

SAMPLE MATERIALS

Self-Assessment Scorecard

Content Understanding Today, we are working on ____________________	I understand ____________________ ____________________ ____________________	I score my *understanding* as _____Great _____OK _____Needs Improvement because ____________________ ____________________ ____________________
Skills The skills I used today were ____________________	I used these skills by ____________________ ____________________ ____________________	I score my *skills* as _____Great _____OK _____Needs Improvement because ____________________ ____________________ ____________________
Participation Today I worked _____Independently _____In a pair _____In a small group	The work I had to complete was ____________________ ____________________ ____________________	I score my *Participation* as _____Great _____OK _____Needs Improvement because ____________________ ____________________ ____________________

Figure 3.5 Self-Assessment Scorecard. *Source*: Author created.

Name____

Today's Topic ____

How do you feel about your learning today?

😄 🙂 🙄 😟 😱

Explain:

____

____

LARGE-SCALE WEEKLY WALL SURVEY

	Knowledge	Skills	Participation
	Developing OK Great!	Developing OK Great!	Developing OK Great!
Monday			
Tuesday			
Wednesday			
Thursday			
Friday			

Figure 3.5 (Continued)

Chapter 4

Professional Development Strategies

This chapter explores the following approaches to professional development (PD):

- Determining how to *Make the Most of PD* (Strategy 16)
- Connecting with others to *Building and Supporting Your Professional Network* (Strategy 17)
- Utilizing *Tech-Based PD* (Strategy 18)
- Engaging in collegial collaboration through *Inquiry Cycles* (Strategy 19)
- Looking back in order to look forward through *Written Reflections on Practice* (Strategy 20)

All of these strategies get to the heart of developing a positive professional disposition geared toward improving oneself in order to provide the best learning experiences for students. This is about working to be the best teacher you can be!

HELPFUL UNDERSTANDINGS

This chapter utilizes larger frames and ideas that you will see referenced often.

Your Professional Development (PD)

Use the UbD (desired results, assessment, and learning plan) framework to think about PD. To make the most of PD, you must know where you want to go with your learning (desired results), you need a way to measure/assess how you are developing as a teacher, and you need to determine how to grow (learning plan).

In the strategies that follow in this chapter, you will read about ways to connect with others within your schools, and through in-person and online professional communities in order to grow professionally.

UbD Highlights

- See step-by-step guidance to help identify your needs and plan for your goals in *Make the Most of PD* (Strategy 16). Get off on the right foot with clear desired results.
- Learn about developing implementation checklists and working with partners for feedback and reflection in *Inquiry Cycles* (Strategy 19). This will help you consider evidence of your professional growth.
- Check out ways to discern online PD sources and to avoid the "time suck" of technology in *Tech-Based PD* (Strategy 18). This will help you ensure your PD action plan is optimal in terms of information and timing.
- See guidelines for reflecting on practice in order to consider how well you are meeting desired results and changes you might make in future action plans in *Written Reflections on Practice* (Strategy 20).

Cultivating a Supportive Climate

Whether working with others in-person or virtually, it is extremely important to have a supportive climate in which you feel comfortable sharing your successes and areas for growth. Hopefully, you are in a school that is supportive of your growth and provides PD that meets your needs. If you need to look beyond your school for professional support, the online resources and suggestions in this chapter for making the most of PD at larger conferences and/or workshops will be helpful to you.

Strategy 17 references Jennifer Gonzalez's famous blog "Find Your Marigold" (2013). In this piece, she explains that when planted beside a vegetable, a marigold helps to protect the "companion plant" and make it thrive. The marigold effect is the impact colleagues can have by supporting you, energizing you, and challenging you. As you read through these strategies, consider how you can work with "marigolds" in your school and larger education networks and how you can provide this kind of support for others.

SUPPORTIVE CLIMATE HIGHLIGHTS

- Check out questions in *Build and Support your Professional Network* (Strategy 17) that help you consider if the colleagues you spend time with are truly building you up professionally.
- Think about how best to represent yourself as an inspiring colleague within your online education community by reading the *Go Viral!* section of *Tech-Based PD* (Strategy 18).
- Think deeply about how to structure feedback by reading *Inquiry Cycles* (Strategy 19).

Reflecting on Reflection

Reflection is a major part of making PD work for you. Take the time to look back at what you have done and apply that experience to where you are headed. Green (2006) writes,

> When a novice [or veteran] teacher can envision teaching and learning from multiple perspectives, that teacher is empowered to make decisions confidently and reflectively. When a teacher believes in her ability to make good instructional decisions, she can be an autonomous, effective professional who can weather the vagaries of education, confident in her vision and professional practice. (p. 6)

Bring your best reflective self to your PD experiences. Stay open to multiple perspectives on experiences and work to apply your deeper understandings that emerge from your teaching, learning, and networking in order to develop the best learning experiences for your students.

GUIDING QUESTIONS

As you read through this chapter, consider the following:

- How do I incorporate the UbD framework (desired results, assessment, learning plan) in my PD?
- Am I working in a climate that is conducive to my professional growth? If so, how can I capitalize on this? If not, what can I do to create a better climate, or where can I connect with positive supports outside of school?
- When asking for feedback from colleagues, what are specific areas of focus that I can suggest and will be open to?
- Is my time spent with tech-based PD platforms worth the investment? Why? Why not?
- How am I embracing both my introspective and interpersonal sides when it comes to PD?
- In what ways can I push myself to think more deeply about my own choices and/or to connect with and learn from others?

STRATEGY 16: MAKING THE MOST OF PD

Chapter Contributors
Cathy Xiong, Robert F Wagner Schools for Arts and Technology (NY), 6th–8th grade
Brittany Klimowicz, NYC iSchool (NY), 9th–12th grade

Professional Development (PD) is a powerful tool to improve teaching pedagogies and to strengthen content knowledge. The goal of PD is to provide opportunities for teachers to improve their practice and learn from each other. However, the goal of PD and the reality of PD are too often disconnected. PD (school based or outside of school) can feel forced, be led by individuals who aren't strong facilitators, or be given as a one-size-fits-all to a diverse teaching staff (in terms of experience, content area, etc.). Therefore, it is important for teachers to know how to find the right PD for them and to make the most of PDs that are offered to them. Finding the right PD is about teachers individually or collectively seeking out new resources and engaging in conversations to share their experiences and offer feedback. Additionally, teachers are able to make the most out of PDs that involve choice, allowing teachers to find support for their specific goals and meeting them at their level of experience.

STRATEGY IMPLEMENTATION

Finding the Right PD (Outside of School)

1. *Identify Your Pedagogical and Professional Needs*—Critically reflect on your pedagogical and professional needs, what you are doing well, and where you need support. Consider:
   - Colleagues or students who can offer insight to your areas of growth
   - The best way to prioritize your pedagogical and professional needs
   - Which pedagogical and professional needs will require outside support
2. *Plan Short-Term Educational Goals*—Based on the pedagogical and professional needs you identify, determine short-term goals you hope to achieve for each identified need. Think about:
   - Goals that are attainable within this school year
   - Steps needed to take to achieve each goal
   - What support and which PDs will help you achieve each goal
3. *Find Potential PDs*—Use your teaching and professional networks to identify potential PDs you can attend. When determining the right PD, keep in mind:
   - Colleagues that have connections to listservs, professional organizations, and/or other PD opportunities that you can access
   - Professional organizations in your area of need that offer PD opportunities
   - Whether your desired PDs can help you reach your planning goals
   - The costs, time commitment, and travel needs for possible PDs
   - If funds are available to attend PDs and if you will have to miss teaching time

4. *Research Potential PDs*—Once you have found possible PD opportunities, take time to determine which PD is the best fit for your needs:
   - Are there people you can talk to who have attended your desired PDs to get their feedback?
   - What information do you need to gather in order to decide whether you should attend a PD?
   - What supports will you have for continuing this learning and implementing next steps in your classroom?
5. *Select One PD to Attend*—Pick one PD and make a commitment to attend. Then determine:
   - *Logistics*—Time off, travel, funding, and so on.
   - *Financial Support*—Look for funding wherever you can to support your PD.
     - *School/District*—Will your school or district provide money to join and attend conferences and PDs?
     - *Selective Organizations*—Are there selective organizations (like *Math for America*) that provide incentives (money and a learning community) for teachers to attend PD in their specific content area, facilitated by master teachers?
   - *Notes*—How should you take notes on things you learn from the PD that you want to implement in your practice?
   - *Materials*—Once at the PD, what materials should you bring home?
6. *Implement What You've Learned into Your Teaching Practice*—When you return to your school after attending the PD, try to immediately implement what you learned into your teaching practice. Consider:
   - *Timing*—When in your teaching practice, within the first week of returning to your school, can you integrate what you learned from the PD?
   - *Implementation*—How can you naturally integrate what you learned into your practice without disrupting the routines, practices, and culture of your classroom (unless major disruption is needed)?
   - *Assess*—What measures can you take to assess and reflect on how well you integrated what you learned?

> Implementation Hint!
>
> Keep yourself committed to implementing what you learned by sending yourself an email or calendar invite at the end of the PD with plans for next steps. That way, when you look at your work email/calendar, you will have a reminder of the great ideas you gathered!

7. *Share with Colleagues/Administration and Ask for Feedback*—Share your learning with colleagues, administrators, and possibly students (depending on the new strategy) and ask for feedback. Think about:
   - The type of feedback you want and need
   - How observers can best provide useful, critical feedback
   - How your own critical reflection can support and extend the feedback you receive from others

8. *Make Modifications Based on Self-Reflection and Peer Feedback*—Be thoughtful and strategic in how you receive and apply feedback about how to strengthen your new strategy. Once you have adapted the strategy based on feedback, try it again (and repeat the feedback/revision process as many times as needed). Ask yourself:
    - After trying the strategy again, does it work better?
    - Can and should I integrate this strategy into my practice moving forward?
    - Do I need to go through a feedback/revision process again?
    - Did the integration of the strategy help me meet my PD goal(s)?

Making the Most of Your PD (In School or Out of School)

1. (In School) *Encourage Administration to Create Choice/Differentiation for PDs*—If your school does not already do this, encourage your administration to provide choice and differentiation for teachers with regard to their PD. This could be done using small group PDs that are facilitated by other teachers facilitated by teachers. When considering small group PD facilitated by teachers, determine:
    - What PDs would be useful for you and your peers
    - Which teachers could facilitate useful/productive PDs for small groups of educators
    - How school PDs might be differentiated to support the needs of each educator
2. *Keep a Positive Mindset*—Recognize that school-wide PD is usually to get everyone on the same page, improve the whole school community, and create a larger school culture. Make sure you:
    - Figure out how the PD is relevant to your teaching (even if you have to be creative).
    - Support colleagues in making the most of each PD.

HOW THIS STRATEGY MIGHT BE ADAPTED BASED ON TEACHING EXPERIENCE

Early Career Teachers

Early career teachers need more support; therefore, try to take advantage of visiting classrooms of veteran teachers you respect to learn from them. This will be a great asset in addition to PDs provided by the school. Finding out-of-school PDs might be overwhelming in your first years of teaching; as a result, take advantage of opportunities to learn from within your school.

Veteran Teachers

Advocate to become a teacher leader who can help facilitate PDs based on your expertise. Work with colleagues and administrators to find and develop PDs that will support your areas of growth. Additionally, engage in mentor relationships with early career teachers who can share new ideas and pedagogy while you support them in myriad ways. Shake up your practice by trying something new and inviting colleagues to observe and give feedback.

STRATEGY IN ACTION: TAKING THE LEAD WITH PD

"I have a unique history with PD. At my previous school, I eventually became a teacher leader that helped plan, run, and co-facilitate our school-based PD program. As a teacher who was concurrently teaching while inhabiting the teacher leader role, I directly felt connected to the work the teachers in our community were doing and the challenges they faced with our student population. We quickly realized when planning PD for such a diverse staff that we needed to provide different supports for different teachers. Sometimes that meant that we strategically grouped teachers by experience level (homogeneous vs. heterogeneous) and sometimes that meant that we provided breakout groups on a particular PD goal. Part of one school year we allowed people to pick which goal/PD group they wanted to be a member of, and then in those small groups, they would work on one specific goal. In general, these moves helped to strengthen our staff's PD experience and created a culture of continued learning. Teacher choice is definitely a helpful part of PD progress. Additionally, my school tries to create a larger culture of continued learning."

—Brittany Klimowicz

WHY I LIKE THIS STRATEGY

"Teachers, just like students, are at different places in their own learning and therefore need different things. Since teachers' non-instructional time is precious, having PD that allows teachers to feel valued and helps them reach their goals will always feel like the best use of time. Additionally, if we really want to impact teaching practices for the better, then we need PD that will appropriately support that. In my opinion, PD serves a number of purposes: being able to provide emotional support for teachers in their learning and growth and to improve the overall pedagogy of the school community."

—Brittany Klimowicz

"We as educators 'learn to teach.' Like any other profession, continuing education should be a constant effort to stay at the forefront of what we teach. Professional development workshops offer great resources and opportunities to connect and collaborate with other teachers."

—Cathy Xiong

Adaptation for Different Assets/Needs

Access to Funding/Resources	
Limited Access	*Lots of Access*
*Find organizations like *Math for America* that support teacher PD. *Get your school to find community partners to "sponsor" teacher PD. *Work with the school's administration to maximize the school's PD funds to best support teachers' needs.	*Take advantage of the resources provided to you, determine which resources will be most useful to your practice, and use the funding you have to seek out new resources that meet your areas of need/growth.
Time Allocated for PD	
Limited Time	*Lots of Time*
*If you are only able to attend in-school PDs, try to take advantage of your prep time to engage in webinars and other remote PDs. *Ask colleagues to share resources from PDs they attend.	*Research relevant PDs you can attend out of school or bring to your school (free and financed). *Share resources with colleagues who have and have not attended the same PDs as you. *Create professional networks you maintain with individuals you meet at PDs.
Opportunities for Collaboration with Colleagues	
Few Opportunities	*Lots of Opportunities*
*Advocate for formal or informal common time built into the school week to allow teachers across departments to collaborate and share resources. *Create a teacher network outside of the school day that allows you to work with teachers from other school communities. These could be teachers from your teacher preparation program, online or social media Twitter communities, or other spaces to collaborate with educators.	*Create team-based PD focus areas that you explore collaboratively. This can be across disciplines and within disciplines and grade levels. *Revisit PD focus areas as new student, teacher, and school needs develop. *Develop systems of sharing and evaluating PD resources with your colleagues that allow you to differentiate and apply various resources to your specific pedagogical needs.

STRATEGY IN ACTION: SELF-DIRECTED PD CYCLES

"It is 3:00 pm on Monday, as usual, teachers in our school gather in the library waiting for an hour-long professional development. Unlike a few months ago, the room is filled with excitement and engaging conversation. So what changed? For a long time, teachers were unsatisfied with the quality of the professional developments offered in the school. Oftentimes, the workshops were irrelevant to what people were teaching. As a result, teachers were dreadful when attending what they saw as useless meetings. Recently, a group of teachers came together and formed a PD committee in an effort to create effective and quality PD in the school. The outcome was Monday PD time has turned to a self-directed PD time. This model allows teachers to explore PDs of their own interests. *Each self-directed PD cycle lasts for four weeks, and at the end of each cycle, teachers come together and showcase their work.*

Some teachers go out of the building to attend lectures; some do online courses; some teachers build their own design; and some teachers work collaboratively. Then, at the end of each cycle, teachers working on similar topics present. There are three cycles per year and some teachers do the same thing for each cycle.

I found this self-directed PD especially helpful for me. This year, I was assigned to teach a new course in computer science. I was extremely nervous because I don't have enough content knowledge. I was able to use a lot of the PD time to look for resources, watch video tutorials, and even attend PD outside the school to strengthen my content knowledge in the field. As a result, I was able to meet many other computer science teachers and learn from experts. The conversations and the share out sessions made me feel supported as a new teacher in this field. I was able to bring back a lot of resources to my own classroom and improve my own teaching practices."

—*Cathy Xiong*

STRATEGY 17: BUILDING AND SUPPORTING YOUR PROFESSIONAL NETWORK

Chapter Contributors
Barry Saide, Roosevelt School (NJ), 4th–5th grade
Meaghan Phillips, Byram Intermediate School (NJ), 5th–8th grade

Blogger Jennifer Gonzalez wrote a famous piece in 2013 about finding your marigold. A marigold is one of the best flowers for companion planting. When planted beside a vegetable, it helps to protect it and make it thrive. The marigold effect is the impact of colleagues who can be supportive of you, energize you, and challenge you. Seek out colleagues who are working to innovate their practice. Help them see that what they are doing is special and learn from one another. Not only will they be marigolds to you, you will be a marigold to them. When you have driven, supportive colleagues as part of your professional community, you will work to demonstrate the same qualities.

STRATEGY IMPLEMENTATION

Part I: Find Your People

1. *Communicate Your Beliefs and Desire for Growth*—Remember that how you communicate your approach to your career as an educator will impact the people who are attracted to working with you. Share:
   - Your passion for being an educator
   - Innovative ideas you are trying/considering
   - Forward-moving ways to respond to setbacks
2. *Find People Who Make You Better*—Ask yourself the following questions to see if you are spending time with people who build you up:
   - Who are you spending time with?
   - What do you admire about these colleagues professionally?
   - Are you comfortable sharing your successes and failures with these colleagues?
   - Do you trust the advice that these colleagues offer?
   - How have your colleagues been supportive of innovations in your teaching?
   - If you need to change the tone of your interactions with colleagues to be more supportive, how can you do so?

> "Collaboration and a strong sense of community are critical elements for any professional academic staff. If you're not careful, teaching can so very easily feel like an island: you're isolated in your classroom, with your students, teaching your subject. You may have a few other islands you occasionally visit, but you're ultimately locked away from the huge potential of the other educators surrounding you."
>
> —*Meaghan Phillips*

Part II: Support Each Other

1. *Stay Connected and Positive*—Keep in regular contact with your PD network. Boost one another up by:
   - Listening when things aren't going well

- Sending emails/texts
- Sharing resources
- Putting aside judgment

2. *Go Beyond the Expected*—Encourage people in your PD network to do more. This can take varied forms:
   - Observe each other's teaching
   - Research best practices
   - Review student data
   - Attend an EdCamp together
   - Write a blog post, article, or chapter for publication
   - Present at a conference
   - Seek funding for something teaching related that matters to you

Is an EdCamp Right for Me?

An EdCamp is a free professional development opportunity that is led by educators for educators. When you attend an EdCamp, you will learn from people who are "walking the walk" because they are classroom teachers who are using the strategies that they share. An EdCamp is also attractive to many teachers because the construct allows for them to feel comfortable leaving a session if it is not applicable to them. At EdCamps, the focus is on making sure your time is working for you. If you leave a session, head to another session or use the time to talk with others who are not in a session.

HOW THIS STRATEGY MIGHT BE ADAPTED BASED ON TEACHING EXPERIENCE

Early Career Teachers

Be a keen observer. Read body language. Discern what is conveyed nonverbally. In a faculty meeting or in a workshop, who is doing the talking? Who is doing the listening? How are people physically postured? Consider how people contribute to the culture of your school or your larger PD community. Who will promote your growth? Connect with those people!

Veteran Teachers

You may feel more comfortable at this point in your career. This can allow you to feel relaxed and confident when challenged. Regardless of who is saying what, if you know what you are doing is right for your students, you can back it up and share your reasoning with others. Continually reflect on your own areas of growth and find the right people to support those areas!

STRATEGY IN ACTION: PINEAPPLE TUESDAY

"Once a month, my school has something called 'Pineapple Tuesday.' On the third Tuesday of every month, grade-level team time is cancelled, and teachers are encouraged to spend approximately 40 minutes visiting another classroom, observing the processes and systems, and the lessons and material. [Pineapples stand tall and wear a crown; therefore, teachers show they are ready to share their strengths by posting a pineapple cutout on their door. This is a symbol that colleagues are welcome to visit and observe.] Visitors jot down their thoughts on a post-it note and set a time to dialogue with the classroom teacher later.

On one particular 'Pineapple Tuesday,' I decided to visit some of my former students in their 8th Grade ELA class. The class was run by a teacher I knew but hadn't interacted much with in the past; we'd had a couple of conversations, and we both were in the ELA Department, but that was about the extent of our professional relationship.

When I got to class, I was immediately struck by the professionalism and maturity that was palpable in the air. By observing a Socratic Seminar process, I was able to see that this teacher, Mrs. H., knew how to go about setting and achieving high standards while also encouraging creativity and innovative thinking. She was so well-suited to taking our students from where they had been at the end of 7th Grade and preparing them for high school. I just had to start picking her brain for tips, tricks, and strategies. We now collaborate and communicate regularly, and I believe that our students greatly benefit from this.

For me, the benefit of 'Pineapple Tuesday' is also much more personal. This practice didn't just put me into contact with a coworker who I could swap lessons with; like me, Mrs. H. is an introvert. Bonding over the struggles and strengths of being an introvert has become a hallmark of our relationship, and I am truly grateful for it.

I'm the type of person who could've very easily remained an island without the proper encouragement. But I can honestly say I'm much, much happier in my bigger, more connected world full of pineapples."

—Meaghan Phillips

WHY I LIKE THIS STRATEGY

"Education is a team sport. When one of us learns something and turnkeys it, all of us benefit. The person turnkeying must master the concept in order to teach it—the highest level of understanding is teaching. The person who coordinated the connection with the professional learning opportunity feels good for doing something of value for someone else. It is a win-win-win."

—Barry Saide

> "Collaboration isn't always easy. One of the most common complaints I've heard about collaboration is how time consuming it can be, which can be true. Sometimes it can be tempting to just 'get it done' on your own. Informed and directed collaboration, however, yields powerful and consistent results that better everyone involved. But you still need the time to do it. So, find a way to make some time. Start off small, but make sure it stays consistent. Build on it over time. Remember, being an island teacher is all well and good when the sun's shining, but the minute you're in for some rough weather, it helps to have a support and resource network to rely on."
>
> —*Meaghan Phillips*

Adaptation for Different Assets/Needs

Time	
Limited Time	*Lots of Time*
*Call a colleague on your drive to or from work. *Engage in a text exchange while getting coffee. *Remember, interactions don't all need to be education based or all that long to be impactful.	*Build your own conference or EdCamp that includes space for networking among colleagues/leaders that have impacted you. *Lead a book group that focuses on the work of one of your favorite writers.
Buy-In	
Limited Buy-In	*Lots of Buy-In*
*Start with a small group of inspiring colleagues and see where you go! Even if your PD community is small, it can be impactful. *Remember that inspiration is everywhere! Stay on the lookout for great ideas! If you like a slogan on a real estate sign, think about how you can use it!	*Start a "Smile Squad" to provide small, continuous staff appreciation and energizing opportunities. From a sweet treat on a Monday morning to an inspiring message in your mailbox, these tiny gestures really grow over time and model camaraderie for students. *Encourage one another to present at a conference or EdCamp. Share your successes and meet more inspiring educators too!

STRATEGY 18: TECH-BASED PD

Chapter Contributors
Barry Saide, Roosevelt School (NJ), 4th–5th grade
Tobey Reed, Attleboro High School (MA), 9th–12th grade

Utilize the abundance of platforms available to you online for networking with fellow educators, learning new ideas, sharing successes, and/or soliciting advice for challenges that you face. Choose the platforms that work best for you, and develop approaches for learning from and interacting with inspiring colleagues in a way that is time efficient while yielding impactful results.

STRATEGY IMPLEMENTATION

1. *Choose Your Source*—There are so many ways that you can use social media to impact your PD. A few of our favorites are as follows:
   - *Twitter*—This social media platform allows users to post brief messages (280 characters), pictures, and links to other sites. The brevity of the individual posts means that you take in ideas quickly and simply. Ways to make Twitter work for you:
     - Choose thought leaders in education to follow and get notifications when they post.
     - Sift through tweets by hashtag (e.g., #mindfulness or #ClassroomMangagement).
     - Jump into chats about topics that matter to you. See https://www.pbisrewards.com/blog/twitter-chats-educators/
     - Share successes and seek advice by posting your experiences.

> "One of the nice things is that when I am doing something in my classroom, I will post it on Twitter and then random other teachers in my school will stop and ask me about it. It allows us to break down walls within our school and certainly outside of school."
>
> —*Tobey Reed*

   - *Blogs*—Blogs are conversational, journal-like posts that are typically longer than tweets. Bloggers update their posts regularly and, on most sites, you can search through blogs by using keywords or scanning titles of the posts.
     - Check out the list of blogs posted by TeachThought: https://www.teachthought.com/pedagogy/52-education-blogs-you-should-follow/
     - Choose your blogs carefully. Be discerning! Read through posts and find bloggers that speak to your professional interests and needs.
     - Consider writing your own blog. You can develop it individually, or team with a group of teachers, in order to balance the workload. If you form a group of four to five educators, you only have to write one blog a month to have weekly posts by the group!

- *Podcasts*—These are blogs for your ears! Rather than reading through posts, you can subscribe to podcasts and download these audio recordings so you can listen to them through your phone or computer. We love the portability of podcasts.
  - Check out the list of podcasts posted by TeacherCast: https://www.teachercast.net/blog/7-edu-podcasts/
  - As with blogs and tweets, be discerning!
  - Think about your intentions for listening. You don't necessarily have to listen to just education podcasts. There are educational moments in all we do! The processes and creativity of topics outside of education may parallel your work in your school

"Some teachers may be the only ones in their buildings teaching a particular course. Using digital platforms can help them connect with others teaching similar content."

—*Tobey Reed*

2. *Maximize Professional Impact*—Social media is notorious for being a major time-suck! Develop habits of efficient media use in order to maximize your time spent browsing, taking in information, and interacting with others. Consider:
   - *Tracking Your Time Spent Utilizing Technology*—You may be surprised by how many hours you spend staring at a screen. So think about:
     - Finding apps to help you keep track at https://safe.becausefamily.org/tools-to-monitor-your-own-screen-time-in-2018/
     - *Prioritizing Notifications*—Another distraction from productivity can be email and instant messaging from social media apps. Turn off notifications for any low-stakes sources of messaging. Set a time to check these each day.
   - *Takeaway vs. Time Spent*—Consider whether the amount of time you are dedicating to sifting through tweets, reading a blog, or listening to a podcast is worth the takeaway. You can figure that out by asking:
     - How much of what you are taking in gets applied within the next week, month, or marking period?
     - How does the resource provide insight when you are engaged in conversation with colleagues?
     - Have you or would you recommend this resource to anyone?

A Flood of Information

"On average, there are 500 million tweets posted each day! This fact emphasizes how the enormity of information to sift through can be overwhelming! Think of tweets and other posts as drops of water in a constantly moving stream. There is no way to see every individual drop. Develop your method for scooping up ideas when you can and examining the ideas you select more fully rather than trying to capture the entire stream of information."

—*Tobey Reed*

STRATEGY IN ACTION: BUILDING ON POTENTIAL

"When I was Director of Curriculum and Instruction in a small, rural school district, I worked with a first grade teacher who had moved into a position as the elementary iSTEM teacher. She was motivated, energized, and consumed everything thrown her way. Having worked with her on writing curriculum for the elementary iSTEM program, I could tell she would take any opportunity and run with it.

With that being said, in the last two years, this teacher did the following:

- Wrote a monthly blog post for Engineering is Elementary (EIE)
- Became a product 'piloter' for EIE
- Wrote multiple blog posts for McGraw-Hill and ASCD
- Presented at multiple state conferences
- Led a group of peers to create an EdCamp in the district
- Collaborated with 4 teachers to write a Gates Foundation grant funded for $27,400

Based on all of the above, this teacher was offered a book deal with a major publisher and was featured by NJEA Monthly Magazine. At the end of the year, this teacher gave me a plaque that read, 'The sign of a good leader is not how many followers you have but how many leaders you create.' She is now a leader in this field. She is the kind of teacher I knew she could be, and she is a teacher leader who will impact how her colleagues work with students in innovative ways!"

—*Barry Saide*

3. *Go Viral!*—If you are using social media as a public relations tool, you want to think about how to get as many eyes on your posts as possible. Be sure that you are posting information that represents the best version of yourself and your school.
   - Represent your best self by asking the following:
     - *Why are you choosing to share this post?* Possible reasons:
       - Promoting great work of your students and/or colleagues
       - Inviting others to join an initiative or event
       - Seeking professional support
       - Sharing a powerful idea/approach
     - *How well does your post represent your intention?*
       - Who/what is the "star" of the post?
       - How might others "push back" against what you are posting?
       - What would your response be to that "push back"?
     - Help your posts "pop" by:
       - Tagging people who will "like," retweet, or blog about your post
       - Using hashtags that are popular in your work

- Developing a few hashtags for your school that are consistently used among your colleagues.
- Remembering that sites like Twitter are quick-moving streams of information. You can adapt and repost tweets several times to get more views.
- Including a quote from books that you are reading, and the author's handle.

HOW THIS STRATEGY MIGHT BE ADAPTED BASED ON TEACHING EXPERIENCE

Early Career Teachers

Discussions about using online tools for PD are now an integral part of new teacher orientation. There are so many resources available to you online, so keep seeking out new tools. Also, you may need to learn how to separate personal and professional use of digital media. Be sure to keep your public online presence professional. Your students and your employers will find you online!

Veteran Teachers

If you are hesitant to try utilizing social media to promote your work and to gather new ideas, get support from other teachers and administrators who are regular users of digital media. Ask them to "like" and repost your posts so you build a following and connect with more colleagues online.

WHY I LIKE THIS STRATEGY

"I can learn so much from educators across the globe without leaving my home. It gives me a great community that tends towards positivity (rare in the social media world). It also enables me to contact experts and get ideas from people who know way more than I do."

—*Tobey Reed*

"I am consistently identifying areas of need in the organizations I am a part of, and I find solutions to those needs by matching my professional learning network members with these opportunities. These opportunities take the form of blog posts by well-known companies/organizations, local/state/national presentation opportunities sponsored by major professional development organizations, advisories to national non-profits and/or Departments of Education, or building my own PD conferences and using my online connections to colleagues to invite them to present."

—*Barry Saide*

Adaptation for Different Assets/Needs

Time	
Limited Time	*Lots of Time*
*Use hashtags to search for topics that matter to you and be discerning about who you follow. *When interacting via social media, use your time wisely. Post or comment while you are waiting in line at the store or waiting to pick up kids from practice. Just don't post or comment while driving!	*Form a team of colleagues who are willing to commit to sharing one great new idea that they found through tech each week. *Set a goal to respond to or "like" five or more posts from your colleagues each week.
Funding	
Limited Funding	*Lots of Funding*
*As you can see by the links that we shared above, there are many websites that can help people learn how to use social media for PD. Use these sites!	*Bring in an expert, or better yet, hire a few teachers to run PD on using technology for PD!

STRATEGY 19: INQUIRY CYCLES

Chapter Contributors
Jeanne Muzi, Slackwood School (NJ), K–3rd grade
Rachel Field Dennis, Morris Academy for Collaborative Studies (NY), 12th grade

Inquiry cycles are multi-week cycles during which groups of educators collaboratively focus on the development of common instructional strategies. Principals, instructional leaders, teacher leaders, and/or teachers identify strategies (using some form of school data) for each cycle based on areas of improvement for teachers and/or students. Each cycle is grounded in collegial collaboration, peer-to-peer observations/feedback/coaching, and critical reflection on the strategy. A new cycle begins once teachers collectively have demonstrated confidence and aptitude in implementing the strategy they've been working on.

WHAT GROUPS OF EDUCATORS SHOULD ENGAGE IN INQUIRY CYCLES?

Inquiry cycles can be carried out with the entire faculty by utilizing professional development time, Professional Learning Communities, grade teams, content department teams, and/or self-selected or appointment groups of educators. The size and nature of the group will likely determine the length of the cycle, the number and scope of peer visitations, and the level of alignment you are looking for in terms of implementation.

STRATEGY IMPLEMENTATION

1. *Select an Instructional Strategy*—Your school's PD team, administrators, instructional coaches, and/or teacher leaders examine school, teacher, and student data to select a strategy that addresses areas of improvement for a majority of teachers and/or students. Strategies often contribute to improving the school and/or classroom climate, empowering students, and moving toward a more student-led classroom environment. When choosing the strategy, consider:
   - What school and student data are most useful in determining a great strategy?
   - Which group of people is best to determine the strategy?
   - How will teachers in your group benefit from working on the selected strategy?

2. *Select a 'Lead Educator' to Model the Strategy*—Determine which teacher or teachers can best model the strategy for the rest of the educators. Then, have the teacher(s) create an implementation checklist that breaks down the components

of the strategy so teachers are in alignment when designing, implementing, and evaluating the use of the strategy. Make sure to:

- Select the best educator(s) to lead this round of inquiry cycles and model the strategy.
- Create a checklist that includes all the necessary strategy components while also allowing for flexibility based on pedagogical styles and classroom contexts.
- Determine how often the Inquiry Cycle group should meet to best go through the entire process.

3. *Introduce Teachers to the Instructional Strategy and Review the Implementation Checklist*—Find a creative way for the lead educator(s) to introduce and model the strategy to the group of educators. Remember:
   - The method of introducing and modeling the strategy will depend on the strategy itself and how involved the rest of the educators need to be.
   - After modeling, debrief the modeling experience and go over the implementation checklist.
4. *Select Inquiry Partner(s)*—Have the lead educator(s), administrators, or teachers themselves select one or two partners. Consider the following types of pairings: veteran with new teachers, co-teachers together, content teachers together, grade-level teachers together, or self-selected. Inquiry partners may remain the same or change every cycle. Consider:
   - Who should determine the inquiry partners?
   - How should partner(s) communicate about progress and hold each other accountable?

THE IMPORTANCE OF CULTIVATING A SCHOOL CLIMATE OF COLLABORATION!

"Through learning walks, coaching, Professional Learning Community meetings, book studies, and teacher-led PD, we have grown as an instructional team as well as practitioners who nurture the Whole Child. Providing time and space for teachers to throw open their doors and welcome colleagues into their classrooms has helped build an environment where teachers can share ideas, get support, and gather feedback. This approach has led to very positive experiences for student teachers and practicum students, as well as growth in teacher leadership through targeted PD, grant programs, and Leaders in Learning projects."

—*Jeanne Muzi*

5. *Create an Individual Plan for Strategy Implementation*—After receiving the implementation checklist and experiencing the model strategy, teachers use their prep time to develop a plan to implement the strategy into a future lesson. Figure out:
   - The lesson in which it makes sense to integrate and try the new strategy
   - If you are staying true to the implementation checklist

6. *Compare and Assess Implementation Plans with Partner(s)*—Before implementing your strategy, meet with your inquiry partner(s) to give feedback on the quality of their plan(s), what will work well, what could be improved, and if each plan is faithful to the implementation checklist. Make sure you think about:
   - The best type of feedback to give your partner(s)
   - How you and your partner(s) can stay true to the implementation checklist and still adapt the strategy implementation to your pedagogical style
   - The next steps each person needs to take to strengthen their implementation of the strategy
7. *Revise Plans as Needed*—Take the feedback from your partner(s) and make any revisions you need in order to maximize the effectiveness of your implementation.
8. *Implement the Strategy*—Teach the strategy in your classroom. Consider:
   - How you can adapt your strategy for your different classes
   - Any changes you might make in the future
   - Successes and concerns that you want to share with your partner
9. *Get Feedback on Strategy Implementation*—Visit others implementing the strategy, have others visit you, and get feedback from your students. Additionally, collect student work from a range of students to assess the effectiveness of implementation across diverse students. Determine:
   - Protocols you should follow for peer observations
   - Types of data you can collect to best assess successful implementation of the strategy

> Feedback Tip!
> Research shows that feedback is most effective when it is focused. Ask your students and your colleagues to provide feedback focused on particular areas of concern for you. For example, you might ask a colleague to note your wait time and your follow-up questioning.

10. *Debrief Visitations*—Use the feedback from your implementation (peer and student feedback) to facilitate critical dialogue with your partner(s) focused on what went well and what you might improve. Plan for a second use of the strategy that integrates what you learned from the debrief. Consider:
    - How you can prepare to take and use critical feedback
    - How you will decide what feedback to take and what feedback won't be useful to you
11. *Follow Up and Repeat Steps 8–10 as Needed*—It is important to revise and adapt strategies as many times as possible by going through the process of trying a strategy, critically reflecting on it, revising it, and trying again. The number of times you do this will depend on how often you can use the strategy, how long it takes to be confident in your effective implementation of it, and the type of feedback you receive from your peers and students.

STRATEGY IN ACTION: SELF-DIRECTED PD CYCLES

"Our school uses inquiry cycles to improve instruction and enhance student outcomes. We know that when students feel successful, credit accumulation, NY Regents exam pass rates, and graduation rates increase, and these strategies not only support student outcomes, but also help teachers to improve their practice. These strategies are designed to be input into our common lesson plan template, which, when used/executed successfully, lead to consistently effective teaching. Our school is unique in that all PD is designed and introduced by our principal each week. It really builds the staff's confidence in his role as an instructional leader and it encourages our instruction to be cohesive. Not only does this benefit the students and staff, but also the outside perception of our school, as we are able to use these strategies when we have outside visits from the superintendent, Quality Reviews, or other guests."

—*Rachel Field Dennis*

HOW THIS STRATEGY MIGHT BE ADAPTED BASED ON TEACHING EXPERIENCE

Early Career Teachers

Be strategic about your areas of growth and advocate to instructional leaders to select strategies for inquiry cycles that align with those areas. Additionally, be proactive about seeking inquiry partners who can best support those areas and make additional efforts to get into classrooms of teachers who have a strong command of the strategies you hope to learn.

Veteran Teachers

Be honest about your areas for growth, and be open to receiving feedback and engaging in critical dialogue with early career teachers.

WHY I LIKE THIS STRATEGY

"This strategy helps to elevate instruction across the school. It ensures that teachers are being mindful about instruction while improving their practice. The common strategies also improve classroom management for struggling teachers and help make the work of the class student-led."

—*Rachel Field Dennis*

"I like inquiry cycles because they incorporate collective efficacy, collegial collaboration, and student engagement/empowerment, which means everyone is rowing the boat in the same direction. Therefore, the focus is on improving as educators, to thus improve outcomes for kids."

—*Jeanne Muzi*

Adaptation for Different Assets/Needs

School/Administration Buy-In	
Limited Buy-In	*Lots of Buy-In*
*The rationale behind the inquiry cycles needs to be solid. Have the instructional leaders be transparent and explicit about how each teacher will benefit from participating in the cycles. Teachers should know what they are doing, why they are doing it, and the ways they can see results (i.e., pass rates, supporting struggling students, etc.). "Teacher needs to feel connected to the work or it doesn't work."—Rachel Field Dennis *Ensure the Lead Educator is someone who will engage all involved.	*Feed off of the energy and find ways to engage different "Lead Educators" throughout different inquiry cycles. *Aim to complete one inquiry cycle during each academic quarter of the school year. *Encourage peer visitations beyond the scope of inquiry cycles.
Timing for Visitations/Meeting	
Limited Time	*Lots of Time*
*Be strategic with scheduling for PDs and visitations so you ensure you are able to, at minimum, meet to see the model strategy, meet once to review implementation plans, and visit one another and debrief. *Meet remotely through video or phone chats.	*Use shared planning/PD time to meet at every stage of the inquiry cycle process. *Conduct multiple peer visits.

STRATEGY IN ACTION: GET INTO ONE ANOTHER'S CLASSROOMS AND SHARE BEST PRACTICES

"I realized that some of my teachers had never been inside each other's rooms, so I held our October meeting in the Pre-K classroom. The Pre-K teacher shared 'Tools of the Mind'—curriculum focused on self-regulation. In the November meeting, Kindergarten teachers gave an amazing presentation on the importance of play (research and practice-based). In the December meeting, 1st grade teachers shared their Orton Gillingham training. Through this sharing and visitation process, teachers realized they no longer needed to exist in their grade-level silos.

It's all about the willingness to open your doors to someone else. Say to one another, 'I will cover your class. You go spend some time in second grade. You are doing reader/writer workshop. Go see how Kindergarten introduces it.' It's so important to see teachers as experts and collectively say, 'we are going to get better.'"

—*Jeanne Muzi*

SAMPLE MATERIALS

Sample Implementation Checklist

- Directions are explicit and include all elements of the strategy.
- Modeling is included in the roll-out of the strategy.
- Differentiation is used to meet the needs of all learners.
- There are formative assessments being used to check for student understanding and skills development while students are engaged in the strategy.
- The teacher is circulating and supporting students as needed.
- The teacher is addressing student questions, concerns, and specific needs.

Figure 4.1 Sample Implementation Checklist. *Source*: Author created.

STRATEGY 20: WRITTEN REFLECTIONS ON PRACTICE

Chapter Contributors
Kimberly Murray, Colegio Karl C. Parrish (Colombia), Kindergarten
Janelle Chiorello, Joyce Kilmer MS (NJ), 8th grade
Kelsey Collins, Livingston High School (NJ), 11th and 12th grade

Take time during or after teaching a lesson to: critically reflect on the effectiveness of the lesson. Note changes to make in scaffolding, strategies, topics, resources, and so on, and consider ideas for upcoming learning experiences. This strategy is focused on critical *written* reflection on practice rather than on-the-spot thinking that enables teachers to change the learning experience in the moment. That said, it is usually important to note the on-the-spot changes that are made when engaging in written reflection.

STRATEGY IMPLEMENTATION

1. *Preliminary Critical Reflection*—Consider the objectives of the unit and the learning experiences that you are developing. Think about:
   - The Knowledge/Skills/Dispositions (KSD) that you want your students to develop
   - How these K/S/D correlate with standards and assessments
   - How the lesson's learning experiences help students meet or exceed the unit objectives
2. *Select Your Mode of Reflection*—Decide which reflection tool(s) will be most useful for you. Possible modes of reflection include: Post-It notes, a writing journal (paper or electronic), and/or making lists of changes for next year. Ask yourself:
   - What is easiest to use while teaching?
   - What is going to give you the space/adaptability that you need to make clear how your reflections correlate with specific parts of your lesson? (e.g., Post-It notes may be placed on the page next to the intended change.)
   - What will you most likely return to, in the future, to implement the changes noted during your critical reflection?
   - Do you need multiple modes of reflection, and if so, how can you get them to work harmoniously?
3. *Reflect along the Way*—Reflect before, during, and after each lesson/unit. Consider the objectives for the day or the larger K/S/D of the unit of study. Use the following questions to guide you:
   - *Before the Lesson*:
     - What K/S/D do you want students to develop today?
     - How do you know that students are developing these K/S/D?
     - How will you know if students are struggling?

- ◦ How can you extend student learning if students have already met the K/S/D objectives?
- ◦ What approaches have been working with students?
- ◦ What new approaches do you want to try?
- ◦ What mode of reflection(s) do you plan to use today?

- *During the Lesson*:
  - ◦ Are students engaged?
  - ◦ How do you need to adapt learning experiences that do not seem to be achieving the desired outcomes?
  - ◦ What supports/extensions would benefit students?

- *After the Lesson*:
  - ◦ What approaches met or exceeded your expectations, and how can you replicate it again in the future?
  - ◦ Have students met your learning outcomes (K/S/D) for the day?
  - ◦ What supports/extensions would benefit students?

> "I don't see how I could be a teacher without doing this, especially with the amount of standards schools are requiring teachers to work with."
>
> —*Kimberly Murray*

- *After the Unit*:
  - ◦ How well did the lessons build on one another?
  - ◦ How successful was your overall unit design in helping students meet the big ideas and K/S/D for the unit?
  - ◦ Do students see the relationships among big ideas in the unit?
  - ◦ How can students transfer the skills that they learned to future units in your class and beyond?
  - ◦ What will you need to incorporate into your next unit in order to reinforce and extend student learning?
  - ◦ What adaptations will you need to make to your unit, lessons, learning experiences, differentiation, and so on when you teach this unit again next year?

4. *Consolidate Notes from Reflections*—At the end of the unit, gather all of the notes you took (electronic, paper, etc.) and organize them in one space you will return to in the future. You should place those notes in a space where you cannot miss them. (We recommend having a digital copy of your reflections in case you lose or misplace any hard copies.) This could be a bulleted list, shorthand annotations, long-form paragraphs, or any other form of concrete reflections for changes you want to make in the future.

5. *Revisit Notes before Teaching Unit/Lesson Again*—When revisiting notes from the previous year, keep in mind that students are unique; therefore, the notes you made last year may or may not apply to your current student population.

STRATEGY IN ACTION: REFLECTION ON WRITING INSTRUCTION

"The first time I really thought about using this strategy was when I was teaching writing. My students were lacking various writing skills, and it showed daily in the overall lesson. Because of this, I decided to become extremely reflective on 'how' and 'what' and 'why' I was teaching a particular skill. At the time, my students struggled with using textual evidence to explain their reasoning or thesis, as well as explaining how the textual evidence relates back to their thesis. At first, I went over methods again and again, and my students still were not producing textual evidence in their writing. I became frustrated until I realized that it could be something that *I* was doing. That's when I decided, *let me comb through the lessons, let me study my execution of the lesson, and then see if there's any way I can relate the content more to my students' lives, so that they could master this skill.* I revamped the lesson and my students benefited from these changes. I used song lyrics and a thesis and again, showed them step by step, the why and the how of using textual evidence. This time, my students got it! They began using textual evidence in an academic sense as well. For me, the biggest takeaway from this experience is that no teacher is perfect. The profession requires us to become reflective on our practices so that we can grow and develop as educators. Using this strategy has helped me become a better teacher for my students."

—*Janelle Chiorello*

HOW THIS STRATEGY MIGHT BE ADAPTED BASED ON TEACHING EXPERIENCE

Early Career Teachers

Focus on both what is going well and what you want to change. Too often, early career teachers are very hard on themselves and fall into the trap of teacher guilt. You might benefit from using the following simple, critical reflection questions: *What went well? What needs to change? How can I make it better?* When you reflect, be sure to consider the needs of special populations (English Language Learners, Special Education students, and Gifted and Talented students).

Veteran Teachers

Look for ways to change and grow in your role. You might choose to focus on a particular area of professional growth in your written reflections. To do so, consider which of the reflection questions in this chapter help you examine challenges you are facing and strengths you have with your particular area of professional growth. How are you sharing those challenges and strengths with colleagues?

WHY I LIKE THIS STRATEGY

"Written reflections on practice allow me to delve deep within myself as an educator. Instead of becoming frustrated with myself that a lesson might not have gone as planned, or that students were just not involved or mastering the skill, I can go back to the lesson and pinpoint what I can do to not only improve my teaching practices, but also to improve my students' learning experience."

—*Janelle Chiorello*

"Written reflections on practice help me ensure that my instruction is effective in keeping students motivated and engaged in learning which supports student progress."

—*Kimberly Murray*

Adaptation for Different Assets/Needs

Opportunities for Collaboration with Colleagues	
Limited Opportunities	*Lots of Opportunities*
*Send an email to ask for support from colleagues who are teaching the same students or similar K/S/D. *Find a reflection buddy. This can be a person you eat lunch with or just check-in with regularly to share successes and challenges. If you don't have time to meet in person, you can communicate via email or just leave materials/plans on which you'd like some support/suggestions in each other's mailboxes.	*Create a template for everyone on your collaboration team to guide their critical reflection (What went well? What do you need to change? How can you make it better?) Ask the team to fill out the template as they finish their unit. *Participate in collaborative meetings (Professional Learning Communities or other meeting formats) to discuss how the unit went. Incorporate analysis of student achievement (Did students meet objectives? Why? Why not?).
Time Allocated for PD/Teacher Prep	
Limited Time	*Lots of Time*
*Quickly reflect on the lesson right after teaching it, or any time before you teach your next lesson, and jot notes down in your journal/notebook/lesson plan/computer. Simply think about what you can change to make the lesson better.	*Use a broader approach to thinking about the unit as a whole, how lessons build on one another, and how individual lessons support larger goals. *Use more than one medium for reflection. You may want to use a teacher journal in addition to notes on unit/lesson plans themselves. *Take time to reflect with colleagues. Gather feedback and support, and share your strengths.

STRATEGY IN ACTION: INDIVIDUAL AND SHARED REFLECTION

"Last year was my first year teaching and honestly it took hindsight for me to realize how I was overwhelmed pretty much all of the time. After teaching my third unit to my freshmen students, I was feeling frustrated because of how long it took me to teach units two and three. I felt as though I had not honed in enough on particular skills or concepts that I wanted to teach them; I felt as if I had been pulled in different directions and was trying to cover too much material. I think I just realized that I needed a release for this frustration, so I wrote down everything that worked with both units and everything that didn't work and how I could change it for the following year.

After doing this individual reflection, I brought up some of the thoughts that I had at an articulation meeting with my fellow 9th grade English teachers. My colleagues were also reflective and passionate educators, so they had their own concerns to bring up as well. This led to a productive discussion about how to streamline and improve our curriculum for the following year. Writing these thoughts down helped me to articulate them clearly in a discussion with others. Once I brought up my concerns to colleagues, I also found it comforting that my colleagues, who had more years of teaching experience, also evaluated their practice each year to try to improve. This validated for me just how valuable it is to reflect, and how this individual practice can be beneficial in a group setting, too."

—*Kelsey Collins*

Chapter 5

Ten Bonus Strategies

In these final pages, you will find ten bonus strategies that require small changes/steps for implementation but make a *huge* impact. Sometimes, teacher candidates and newer teachers benefit from having these "teacher moves" made explicit. For more seasoned teachers, some of these strategies may seem like "teacher moves" that are second nature, and if that is the case, hopefully seeing them on this list serves as an affirmation of good practice!

1. *Greeting Students at the Door*
   Do your best to be ready for class so you can stand at the door and greet your students as they walk in. Some teachers have options for choosing greetings (high five, fist bump, handshake). Simply greeting students by name and looking at their body posture and facial expression can give you a good sense of students' readiness for learning and help you connect with students for the day. If you work in a school where you move from classroom to classroom and need the time between periods/blocks to set up your lesson, try to greet the students verbally as they enter while you are preparing your room.
2. *Grounding*
   So often teachers are rushing from one task to another in an attempt to get as much as possible crossed off their "To Do" list. Students are rushing from one class to another, thinking about their after-school activities, balancing family and friends, and just trying to squeeze in some time for fun! To get yourselves settled before starting class or moving into a new topic, try some grounding exercises. Take a deep breath together; ask students to take a moment to think about what they are going to do next; connect with a quote or song lyric that gets students (and you) feelling centered and ready to learn.
3. *Lesson Beginnings (Openings, Starters, Warm-ups, Do Nows)*
   However you begin your lesson, it is important that you are deliberate in preparing students to open their minds to the thinking and doing that will take place in the class. Lesson Beginnings are best when they are brief (approximately 5 minutes) and overt in connection to the day's learning. Pose a question that gets students

wondering or debating, share a quote that relates to the kind of thinking or dispositions students will need for the day, show a picture that relates to the day's learning and ask students to respond. Your lesson beginning should be something that *every student* can do (even those who missed previous lessons) and that engages students in thinking about the content for the day. Whatever you choose, be sure to make a clear transition from the opening into the main learning experiences of the day. Also, remember that sometimes lesson beginnings take place several minutes into class time if you have class business to take care of.

4. *Transitions*
   There are two types of transitions: verbal and physical. Verbal transitions help students know how each activity is connected. Make these transitions clear by sharing how students' Knowledge/Skills/Dispositions are developing between each activity and throughout the lesson. Physical transitions involve movement within or outside of the classroom. If your transition requires movement or cleanup, have instructions on the board, and make it clear verbally what students need to do. These physical transitions get easier for students the more often you do it and the more clearly you set expectations.
5. *Microstructures*
   When planning any activity, think about every little detail that is required to make the activity run as smoothly as possible. Common structures to consider when planning an activity include: how the activity is chunked into small parts, how much time should be given to each chunk, who is doing what during each part of the activity (roles), what materials are needed, how are students interacting with one another, and what are you doing as the teacher during the activity. The key to effective microstructures is ensuring that you have thought of as many details as possible before students start the activity *before* they start the activity. Then, your main job is to help students hold themselves accountable to those structures throughout the duration of the activity.
6. *Instructions Three Ways*
   Effective instructions can make or break the success of an activity. Too often teachers think their instructions are clear, but students miss an important point, are confused by something, or just aren't paying attention. As a result, teachers spend so much time re-explaining the activity's instructions when students should have already been working, and the activity, and the activity ends up taking significantly more time than planned. Therefore, it is critical to spend more time up-front going over instructions. Consider giving *instructions three ways*: verbally, posted on the board/projector, and individually for the students (handout or on the computer). Be sure you have 100 percent attention before you give instructions. Then, ask students to reinforce what they have to do by explaining the directions in their own words and asking any clarifying questions. (And if doing a group activity, consider giving the full class instructions before students get into groups, which will reduce chatter about groupings and within the groups.)
7. *Body Positioning*
   When a student is talking to the whole class, keep your body turned toward that student, and move *away* from the student so they have to project their voice

enough for you and others to hear; since students typically "talk to the teacher," it will appear the student is speaking to the whole class and not just you. Also, when you are at the board or in front of the room, as much as possible, keep your body turned toward your students and be sure to turn toward them when talking. No talking into a board! Lastly, when circulating the room during group work, position your body so you can see the rest of the class while engaging individual students or small groups. This will help you see when students have questions, need support, are off-task, or just need encouragement!

8. *First Rate Feedback*
   When you are providing feedback to students *and* when you want feedback from students and colleagues, be sure to provide specifics. It may seem nice to write "good job" on a paper, but that bears little meaning. Rather, tell what parts were strong (e.g., *I really like how you used vivid language to create the image of . . .*). Let students know what you will be looking for in their work (e.g., *I will be looking at how you use evidence to support your claim*). Keep your focus on what you have stated you would look for. Yes, you can line edit a paper or focus on minute details; however, if you and your students agree on focused, pointed areas for feedback, your students' effort and your time providing feedback will be better directed. The same goes for when your students or colleagues are providing you with feedback! Let them know what you are trying to accomplish and areas where you need further direction. This will yield feedback that is meaningful and that leads to next steps.
9. *Reading for PD*
   There are so many great reads for Reading for Professional Development (PD). Remember that, in addition to accessing PD via blogs and other social media, there are journals with excellent teacher-friendly, practical articles, and some excellent books coming out each year that are inspiring. Consider creating a teacher reading group. Meet each month to discuss a book or an article. Focus on sources that provide you with active next steps that you can take into your classrooms.
10. *Someone to Vent to . . .*
   As coauthors, colleagues, and friends, we work together a lot. Not only do we spend time collaborating on our writing and thinking about how to make our courses and PD as great as we can, we spend time just venting to one another! Having a person to vent to is incredibly important. It means that you can "get it out and move on." Sometimes moving on can take some time; but without the venting, it would take even longer! Be there for your colleagues, and try to help the venting transition into positive next steps. That leads to our BONUS Bonus Strategy!

BONUS Bonus Strategy! *Someone to Brag to . . .*

Share your success and journey with these strategies with colleagues and the toolbox community at Website: https://buildyourteachingtoolbox.com/, Email: buildyourteachingtoolbox@gmail.com, Twitter: @BuildTeachTool, Instagram: @buildteachingtoolbox, TikTok: @buildteachingtoolbox, Facebook: Build Your Teaching Toolbox.

Conclusion

This book was developed as a resource that would be useful for *all* teachers in *all* settings. Hopefully the details put into the step-by-step description of strategies throughout the book help you to consider how to implement, or adapt and then implement, strategies that will benefit you and your students.

NOW WHAT?

Remember, the goal is for you to take a Culturally Responsive/Sustaining approach to utilizing these strategies. To do this, ask yourself:

- What do I know about my students?
- How can I adapt these strategies to best fit my students' learning needs?

Further, be sure to integrate these strategies with clear intention and explicit explanation of why you are doing what you are doing. Be brave! Being a bit vulnerable and sharing with students that you are trying something new takes courage. Sharing the *why* behind what you are doing will help students get on board with you, and more importantly, help them think critically about their learning and what works for them. This will also help you to integrate these strategies into your teaching more smoothly than if you simply just insert something new without explanation.

After trying a new strategy, be sure to take the time to reflect.

- What worked well?
- Why did these elements succeed?
- What changes might you make?
- How could you adapt the strategy to better fit your needs or your students' needs?

Most strategies will need to be adapted in some way to fit your classroom. Hopefully the adaptations listed in each strategy are helpful in guiding your thinking. You might consider applying an adaptation from one chapter to a strategy in another chapter. If you are struggling with how to change a strategy, reach out to a colleague, ask your students, or connect with fellow educators at Website: https://buildyourteachingtoolbox.com/, Twitter: @BuildTeachTool, Instagram: @buildteachingtoolbox, TikTok: @buildteachingtoolbox, Facebook: Build Your Teaching Toolbox.

AND THEN?

Practice! Practice! Practice! How do you get better at anything? You practice! Practice new strategies until you feel confident using them in your classroom. Practice adapting strategies for varied learners and varied content. Practice reaching out to colleagues for support, advice, or to be cheered on for your efforts.

Perhaps you are reading this book and thinking, "Hey! I've got some great strategies that can be adapted for varied classroom settings! How do I get my ideas in a book?" Glad you asked! Please, join the toolbox sharing community at Website: https://buildyourteachingtoolbox.com/, Email: buildyourteachingtoolbox@gmail.com, Twitter: @BuildTeachTool, Instagram: @buildteachingtoolbox, TikTok: @buildteachingtoolbox, Facebook: Build Your Teaching Toolbox.

Following the publication of this first book, there are four more books in the Building Your Teaching Toolbox Series! Each book will focus specifically on a different key area of teaching:

1. Classroom Climate
2. Planning
3. Instruction
4. Professional Development

As with this first book, each subsequent book will include step-by-step instructions for implementing/applying the strategy, narratives of the "Strategy in Action," teacher explanations of why they like each strategy, examples of how to modify the strategy based on related assets and needs, modification based on where you may be in your career (early career/veteran), what grade level you teach (elementary, middle, high), and different populations of students (Special Education, English Language Learners, and Gifted and Talented).

In addition to creating a book that could be a strong resource for teachers in varied settings and at different points in their career, this book was written with the hope that it would draw you in as readers and help you feel like a part of a larger community of educators who are eager to share and grow together. Please keep the community growing by providing feedback and new ideas at the email address, website, or social media platforms for the "Building Your Teaching Toolbox" community listed above. Thank you for joining the toolbox community!

References

AHS ILT. (n.d.). *Twitter for educators*. Retrieved June 9, 2021, from http://ahsilt.weebly.com/twitter-for-educators.html

ASCD [@ASCD]. (2019, March 16). *Students have to Maslow before they can Bloom. - @TeachMrReed #Empower19* [Tweet; thumbnail link to video]. Twitter. https://twitter.com/ascd/status/1106937108940406789?lang=en.

Association for Supervision and Curriculum Development. (2007). *The learning compact redefined: A call to action*. http://www.ascd.org/ASCD/pdf/Whole%20Child/WCC%20Learning%20Compact.pdf

Baloche, L. (1998). *The cooperative classroom: Empowering learning*. Prentice Hall.

Bloom, B. S. (1956). *Taxonomy of educational objectives, handbook I: The cognitive domain*. David McKay Co Inc.

Davis, J. R. (2017). *Classroom management in teacher education programs*. Palgrave Macmillan.

Gay, G. (2010). *Culturally responsive teaching: Theory, research, and practice*. Teachers College Press.

Gonzalez, J. (n.d.). *Find your marigold: The one essential rule for new teachers*. Cult of Pedagogy. Retrieved October 12, 2017, from www.cultofpedagogy.com/marigolds/

Green, K. (Spring 2006). *No novice teacher left behind: Guiding novice teachers to improve decision-making through structured questioning. Penn GSE Perspectives on Urban Education, 1*(4): 1–9. Retrieved from www.eric.ed.gov/PDFS/EJ852617.pdf.

Jason G. I. (2007). Ethnic and Urban Intersections in the Classroom: Latino Students, Hybrid Identities, and Culturally Responsive Pedagogy. *Multicultural Perspectives, 9*(3): 21–28. DOI: 10.1080/15210960701443599.

Ladson-Billings, G. (1995). Towards a culturally relevant theory of pedagogy. *American Educational Research Journal, 32*, 465–491.

Lampert, M. (2001). *Teaching problems and the problems of teaching*. Yale University Press.

Lasic, T. (n.d.). *Maslow before bloom*. Human Edublogs. Retrieved July 10, 2020, from https://human.edublogs.org/2009/08/11/maslow-before-bloom/

Maslow, A. H. (1943). A theory of human motivation. *Psychological Review 4*(50): 370–96.

Miller, J. (n.d.). *Gotta "Maslow" before you "bloom"*. The Educator's Room. Retrieved July 10, 2020, from https://theeducatorsroom.com/gotta-maslow-bloom-2/

New America. (n.d.). *Understanding culturally responsive teaching.* Retrieved August 7, 2020, from https://www.newamerica.org/education-policy/reports/culturally-responsive-teaching/understanding-culturally-responsive-teaching/

Paris, D. & Alim, H. S. (Eds.). (2017). *Culturally sustaining pedagogies: Teaching and learning for justice in a changing world.* Teachers College Press.

Robinson, K. (2006, Feb.). *Do schools kill creativity?* [Video]. TED. https://www.ted.com/talks/sir_ken_robinson_do_schools_kill_creativity?language=en

Robinson, K. The Element: How Finding Your Passion Changes Everything. New York: Penguin, 2009.

Schmuck, R. A. & Schmuck, P. A. (2001). *Group processes in the classroom.* (8th ed.). McGraw-Hill.

Stahl, R. (1994). *Using "think-time" and "wait-time" skillfully in the classroom.* (ED370885). ERIC. https://files.eric.ed.gov/fulltext/ED370885.pdf

Stein, J. (n.d.). *Using the stages of group development.* Retrieved June 1, 2021, from https://hr.mit.edu/learning-topics/teams/articles/stages-development

TeacherVision Staff. *Your secret weapon: Wait time, teaching methods and strategies.* Retrieved May 30, 2021, from https://www.teachervision.com/teaching-methods/new-teacher/48446.html

Tomlinson, C. A. & McTighe, J. (2006). *Integrating differentiated instruction & understanding by design: Connecting content and kids.* ASCD.

Wiggins, G. & McTighe, J. (2004). *Understanding by design professional development workbook.* ASCD.

Index

Page numbers in *italics* refer to figures and tables.